CANVAS WORK

Jennifer Gray
CANVAS WORK

B. T. BATSFORD LIMITED   LONDON

ISBN 0 7134 4769 9

Typeset by Servis Filmsetting Ltd, Manchester
and printed in Great Britain by
Anchor Brendon Ltd, Tiptree, Essex
for the publishers
B T Batsford Limited
4 Fitzhardinge Street,
London W1H OAH

Contents

Acknowledgment

I would like to thank Professor
M C Bradbrook, Mistress of Girton
College, for permission to photograph
the hassocks and kneelers in the
chapel; past students Ida Russell,
Joyce Bakes, Mrs Howianz and
Gwendolin Strafford for permission to
photograph their work; James Neil
ARCA for permission to use *Fish Shop*
by Wendy Shearman; Moyra McNeill
for permission to use *Aerial View*;
Wendy Greenfield for permission to use
details of *Owl*; and all the workers of
the Girton College Chapel scheme
whose work has been illustrated in this
book, particularly Anne Clark-
Hutchinson.

The books mentioned in the biblio-
graphy at the end of the book I found
of great help in preparing *Canvas Work*,
and I would like to thank the authors
for some stitches with which I was not
familiar. Some I had known by other
names, and in these cases I have
included all the different names. Some
of the stitches I have invented over the
years, some have been suggested by
seeing new stitches. I should be
interested to know of any others, for it
seems to me one of the richest fields for
invention.

Introduction

Canvas work and embroidery are becoming increasingly well known crafts. More use is made of their variety of stitches than was the case only thirty years ago, when most 'tapestry' work (as it was erroneously known) relied on a limited range of stitches including tent, cross, gobelin and florentine. Even then each piece of work was usually restricted to one type of stitch. The richness and depth that can be produced by the variety of stitches in canvas work, together with the many different types of yarn, lends itself to wall coverings (the original meaning of tapestry) and panels. But it can also be used in many other ways; its hard wearing quality makes it suitable for articles such as bags and sandals, as well as upholstery and rugs. The great improvement in the range of dyes for wool, silk, rayon and cotton means that the work is no longer limited to traditional tapestry colours. Nor does the worker need to go to the other extreme by using crude garish yarns as was unavoidable in Berlin wool work (a 19th century form of canvas work) where the materials used were acid dyed.

This book is to a certain extent a revised version of *Canvas Work and Design* but has taken on a rather different character, concentrating more on stitches and their use in design and less on general ideas for design. As in the previous book the making-up of articles is not discussed.

The first section deals with equipment, including needles, the transferring of the design and the use of graph papers, the framing of work in square (slate) frames and the stretching of finished work. The second section discusses various types of canvas available, their merits and disadvantages. The third section deals with a variety of yarns suitable for canvas work, and shows how stitches later described can obtain different effects when used with different yarns. The fourth section suggests various sources for design and shows interpretations of some of these by embroidery designers.

The major part of this book is devoted to stitches and their interpretation. In some illustrations the canvas on which the stitch sample has been worked is also shown, helping to make the construction of the stitch easier to follow. Other illustrations show stitches which are part of a piece of work, so that it is possible to see what modification is necessary when different stitches meet at the boundary of their areas.

An attempt has been made to correct mistakes made in my previous book, and I hope that this one will encourage further experiment in the design and craft of canvas work.

Preparation for canvas work

EQUIPMENT

The use of the correct equipment for this work will prevent problems such as warped canvas and matted stitching. A general list is given below:

Square (slate) frame
To prevent the canvas warping when stitches are worked on it. A square frame is advisable for soft canvas, since a round one can distort the weave.

Indian ink and fine hog brush
For transferring the design onto the the canvas, or *waterproof felt pen*, for example *Pentel* or *Staedler*, both of which can be obtained in various colours.

Scissors
One large, heavy pair for cutting canvas; one smaller pair for yarns.

Stiletto
For separating canvas threads for eyelets. Scissors can be used instead if they are kept closed whilst entering the canvas and then opened out to increase the size of the hole.

Knitting needle or gauge
For making even loops for tufted stitches.

Set square and ruler
For squaring up when finally stretching work.

Drawing pins (thumbtacks) and board
For stretching work.

Tapestry needles
These have blunt tips which do not split the yarn when stabbed into a hole already containing a stitch. The size of the hole in the canvas and that of the yarn dictate the size of the needle. The eye should be large enough to prevent any wear on the yarn at this point when it is pulled through the canvas, but not so large that it opens out the canvas threads. The needles shown here do not comprise the whole range, but sizes 26 to 22 are useful in the finer range of canvas, 20 to 18 in the middle range and 16 to 13 for the heavier canvasses. Yarns of approximately the same thickness as that shown can be used in the appropriate needles.

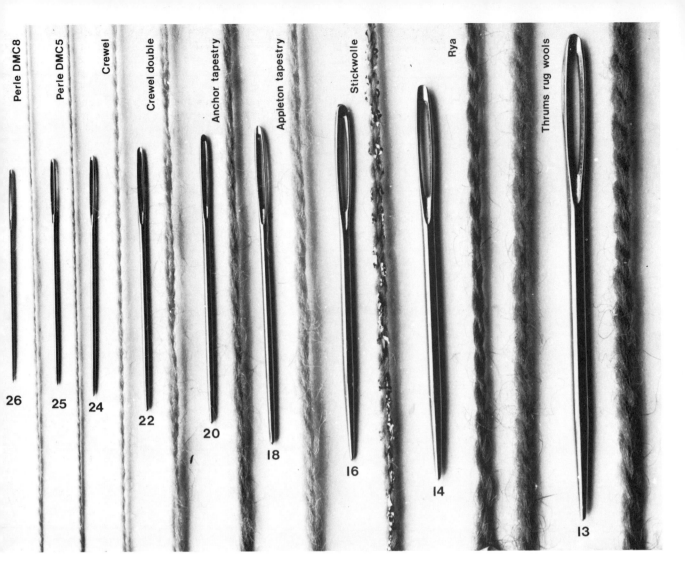

Perle DMC8   Perle DMC5   Crewel   Crewel double   Anchor tapestry   Appleton tapestry   Stickwolle   Rya   Thrums rug wools

26   25   24   22   20   18   16   14   13

TRANSFER OF DESIGN
Painting

One of the simplest, most direct and trouble-free ways of transferring design onto canvas is to trace through from a boldly drawn original onto the canvas with a waterproof felt pen or waterproof ink (not necessarily black), using a fine hogs hair brush. Certain felt pens tend to 'bleed' when the work is damped and stretched, so these should be tested, first by steam ironing and then sponging, to see if the line remains fast. Those recommended are permanent.

If the inked canvas is compared with the original design, it will be seen that the finer lines have been left out and only the main areas drawn in. Where fine lines suggest form (as with the ears of corn), these are often best interpreted by using a stitch suggested by the form rather than a close copy in tent stitch, producing a 'painting in yarn' of the original. For example, an interpretation with 'knobbly' stitches for the corn and sweeping diagonal or straight movement for the leaves would be exciting and interesting. The designing process does not stop at the drawing stage; the choice of yarn, colour and stitch are of equal importance.

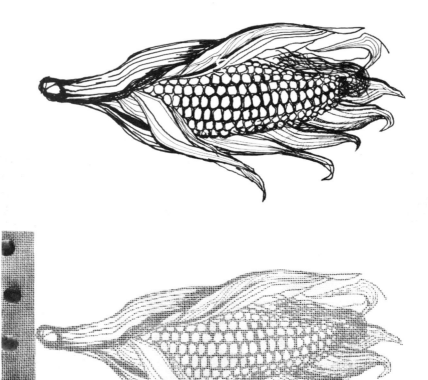

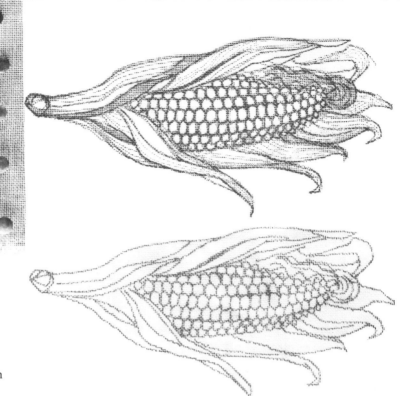

If the design has to be enlarged or
reduced, the original and the canvas
can be squared-up and the design then
painted freehand on the canvas,
copying the original.

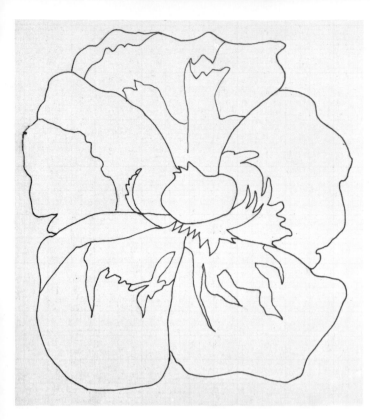

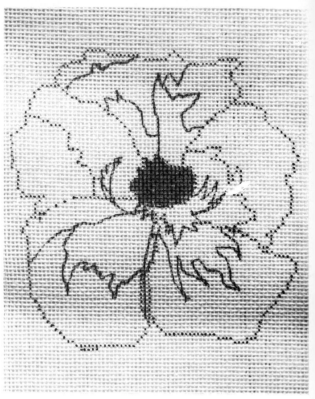

Graph paper
Can be used to transfer a design onto canvas. The lines of the graph paper represent the threads of the canvas, so that the exact position of each stitch can be worked out beforehand. The disadvantage of this method is that it tends to be limiting to the design and usually results in a 'squared' appearance, as half stitches are difficult to indicate. There may also be a tendency to restrict the number of different stitches because of the necessity of drawing them or a symbol for them. Using this method, the symbol is drawn in the square, and it can be difficult to determine whether the lines or the squares of the graph paper represent the threads of the canvas.

This technique can be used in a less restrictive way by drawing the shapes of the design freely on graph paper, and where the line touches a vertical or horizontal line on the grid, marking the corresponding thread of canvas with a dot. This can become tiring on the eyes when used with fine canvas.

Duplicates can easily be made from the original if a number of similar pieces of canvas are required, as for church hassocks. In this case the stitch can be indicated by drawing just one in its area. It is also useful when enlarging or reducing since it eliminates the squaring-up of the original design, which can either be drawn directly onto the graph paper or on paper thin enough for the grid to show through.

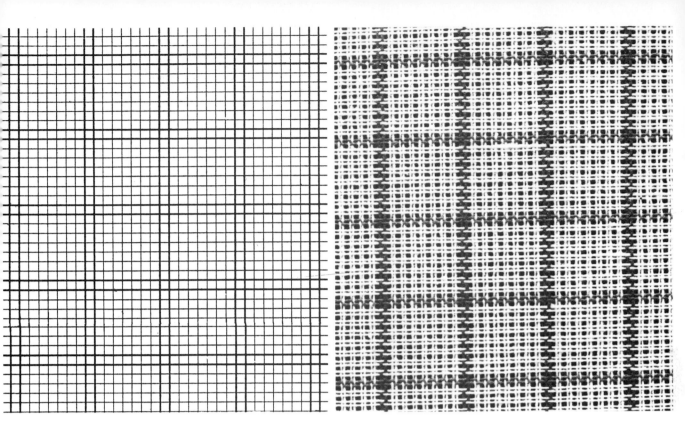

Grid graph paper
An improvement on plain graph paper, since it is specifically designed for use with canvas. It is marked with a double dark line every 8 threads and is intended for use with a grid marked canvas which is slightly coarser than the graph paper. To work actual size double 10s or single 18s canvas can be used, since the 2·5 mm ($\frac{1}{10}$ in.) squares of the graph grid equate with two threads of canvas. To work larger than the grid, coarser canvas should be used while following the same ratio of squares to threads, and a finer mesh canvas will produce a smaller design. Single 10s will increase the design twice size, to reduce the working size by a quarter, 28s should be used.

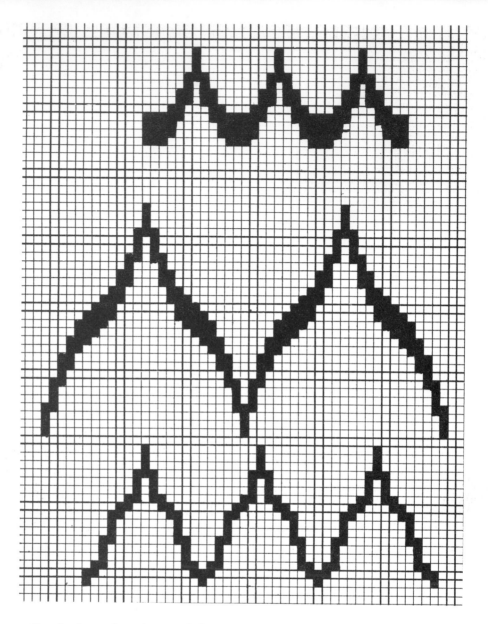

One final use of graph paper is for
the design of florentine and hungarian
grounds when the proposed patterns
can be quickly worked out before being
stitched. The working out of more
complex stitch patterns is best done
directly with yarn on canvas. The first
two patterns are florentine, the third is
hungarian.

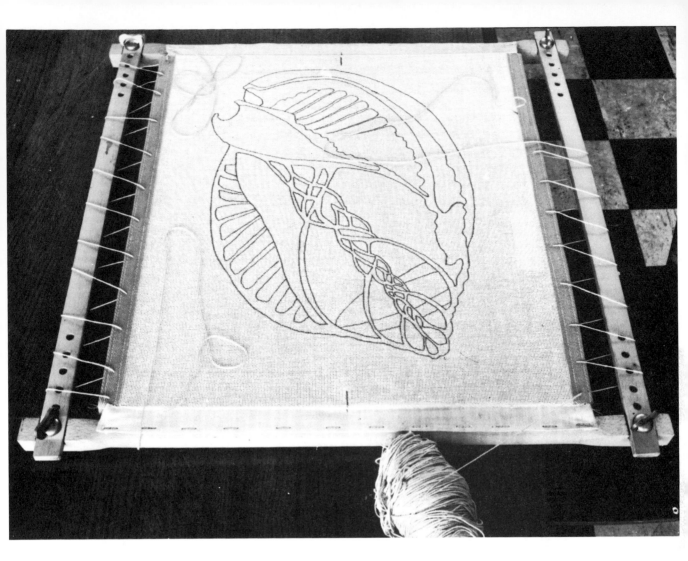

FRAMING IN A SQUARE FRAME

After the design has been transferred
to the canvas, two of the edges (not
those which are to be attached to the
webbing of the frame) are bound and
machined with two rows of stitching
12 mm ($\frac{1}{2}$ in.) apart. The first unbound
edge is then turned under, the centre
marked and placed to the centre of the
webbing (which should also be
marked), so that the two under surfaces

can be pinned together, facing each
other. Overcast from the centre to
both outside edges with strong yarn
or double cotton thread with short
stitches, 1·5 mm ($\frac{1}{16}$ in.) apart. With
coarser canvas 1 stitch in every hole
will probably be sufficient. When the
other edge has been attached in the
same way, the side supports of the
frame are inserted and pegged at the
top edge. The other end is then pulled

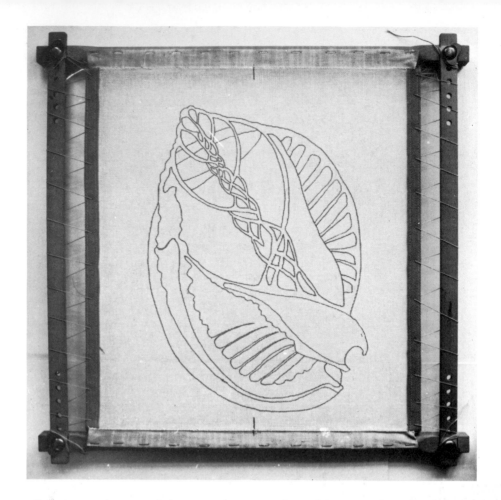

until the canvas is taut and the peg can be placed in the hole. If the canvas is longer than the frame, the spare canvas can be rolled round the lower edge of the frame until the pegs or split pins can be placed in a hole in the side supports. Later when the work is completed on the stretched canvas, the unworked canvas can be unrolled and the excess can be rolled round the upper support. Twine or string is stitched through the taped edges of the canvas between the two rows of machine stitching and round the side supports, about 50 mm (2 in.) apart. When both sides have been stitched with string, this is pulled up evenly on both sides so that the canvas is not pulled towards one support more than the other. The excess string is wound round the end of the frame leaving a loop which can easily be loosened to retighten the canvas.

Seedhead, Jennifer Gray
The centre is emphasised by its strong dark tones of red and brown, while the leaves round it are worked in subtler browns, creams and fawns. This is worked on raffia canvas in thrums, Rya rug wool, Perlita, knitting wools and stranded cottons. The background is flecked bricking. This was drawn directly onto the canvas from a squared-up, smaller drawing and the seedhead itself.

STRETCHING FINISHED CANVAS WORK

It is worth damping and stretching all work when finished even if it has been worked on a frame. It restiffens the canvas, ensures that it is square, and brings the stitching up crisp and fresh. Place two sheets of photographic blotting paper, which is tough, heavy and does not fluff, onto a board. Onto this, with the aid of a set square and ruler draw a right-angled figure the full area of the canvas, taking the two measurements from across the centre of the canvas rather than from the edges. Damp the blotting paper thoroughly and place the embroidered canvas face up in the centre of the drawn shape. Pin down the centre of the top edge and both corners, do the same at the bottom edge and then pin the centre of both sides. More drawing pins can be placed approximately 25 mm (1 in.) apart first along the top edge, then the bottom and sides, making sure that the canvas is not stretched outside the marked line.

The moisture from the blotting paper will slowly evaporate through the canvas and yarn, tightening and shrinking both. Allow the canvas to dry at warm room temperature, for about twelve hours, but do not unpin before it is thoroughly dry. Tape can be stitched on the two unbound edges to prevent scalloping of the canvas threads, but if the pins are close enough together this may not be necessary.

Canvas

Canvas for this type of work is constructed in plain weave with an open ground, that is with one or more spaces left in the reed between warp threads and the weft woven with the same type of spacing. As many as eight embroidery threads (for most stitches) can be contained in one hole without distorting the weave.

STIFF CANVAS

This is treated with size, which seals and stiffens the threads at some stage in its construction. It is either woven with grouped warp and weft threads, grouped warp and single weft threads or single warp and weft threads.

French canvas

Has the warp and weft threads sized before weaving. It is steamed as soon as it comes off the loom to encourage the weft threads to remain in the position in which they are woven. Double canvas is woven in groups of two (not double threads) in the warp and weft, so that where they meet the four threads interweave and form a stable, though open, cloth. The weft is woven initially in the same grouping and spacing, but by the time some of the canvases come off the loom the space between the warp threads has often evened out, producing the appearance of a single warp. This can become slightly confusing when working, but is of advantage where single threads form part of the construction of the stitch. The double threads can slide apart when necessary, but in certain cases this movement of the thread can prove rather unstable, as the tension of the stitching yarn can pull the canvas threads together, producing a malformed stitch.

English canvas

Sized after it comes off the loom and has the advantage over the French in double canvas of retaining both the weft as well as the warp grouping. It produces a very stable cloth which does not warp as easily as the French canvas when worked in the hand. If, however, the ground was out of true when sized, that is warp and weft threads not at right angles to each other, it can prove difficult to pull square. The sizing of the cloth in this way produces a roughness which tends to fray the working yarn more than French canvas but this can be overcome by using shorter lengths of wool or cotton. The problem of dividing the grouped threads when the stitch demands it is a little more difficult than with the French canvas. Single canvas, however, sized in this way rather than by the French method, is ideal for panels and hangings as the threads stay in position, provide a useful stiffening and prevent the canvas from warping too much. French canvas being rather softer is more suitable for articles such as bags and upholstery.

NAME	TYPE	THREADS TO 25 mm (1 in.)
Old Glamis Lauder linen gauze	open weave	32
Dryad Willow cross stitch	close weave	30
Glenshee even-weave	slightly open weave	28, 27, 24
Dryad coarse Willow cross stitch	close weave	18
Danish coarse linen scrim (similar to Winchester)	slightly open weave	18
Old Glamis linens	close weave	19–13

SOFT CANVAS

This is any evenly woven cloth with either some natural stiffness in its make-up from the nature of its fibre, as in linen, or an artificially introduced 'dressing', a starchy substance applied to the fabric after weaving which generally disappears when washed. These fabrics allow the embroidered cloth to drape for curtains or dress. Ground left showing will often enhance and make an interesting background for stitches, especially on cloth of grouped weave.

Grouped weaves

Include Hardanger, a double thread in warp and weft with the space of one thread between; Jute embroidery cloth, also with a double thread in warp and weft but no space left between; and Dobby cloth, a rayon and cotton cloth woven in groups of 4 threads, with 4 holes of the same width to 25 mm (1 in.).

Frame up these fabrics in a square rather than a round frame as the latter tends to open up the mesh of scrim fabrics when it is tautened, leaving an obvious ring mark when the frame is removed. They can, however, be used very successfully if care is taken with the tension of stitches. Some of the more closely woven fabrics like the mercerised cottons (Willow cross stitch) may restrict the use of certain stitches but experiments can be made to discover the full potential of these fabrics. The unevenness of some of the linens may give a slight variation in size of stitch, which could prove a disadvantage or, on the other hand, be utilised in the design.

Canvases available from a number of embroidery suppliers listed at the end of the book, range from fine French canvas 32, 28 and 24 single threads to 25 mm (1 in.), through medium sized French and English canvases between 22 and 14 threads (grouped and single) and coarser canvases of 13 threads, to rug canvas which contains 4 holes to 25 mm (1 in.). A few are illustrated on the following pages, showing double cross stitch worked in yarns suitable for the size of canvas.

The number by which canvas is distinguished relates to the number of threads or tent stitches in 25 mm (1 in.), the 's' or 'sts' still being retained by suppliers to indicate this. The weft threads are always counted and when ordering by post, discover whether the supplier refers to double or single threads in grouped thread canvases. Diana Springall's method of counting holes for double canvas overcomes this problem. A brief description is given, together with the colour and width.

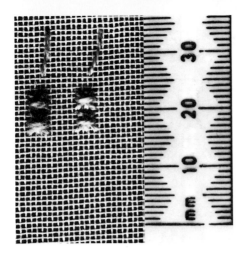

Fine French single: 32s, 28s: crisp
mesh, light orange: 60 cm (24 in.)

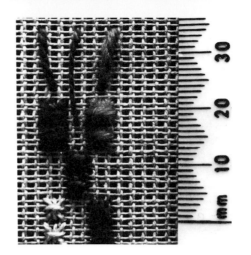

French double: 24s, 12 holes (double
French): stiff grouped warp and weft,
natural: 65 cm (25 in.)

Fine French single: 24s: crisp mesh,
light orange: 60 cm (24 in.)

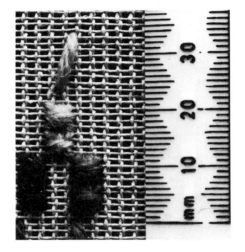

French double: 22s, 11 holes (double
French): stiff grouped warp, single
weft, natural: 65 cm (25 in.)

21

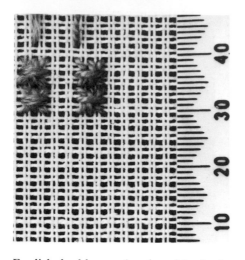

English double: 10s (20 threads): sized, evenly grouped warp and weft, cream: 70 cm (27 in.)

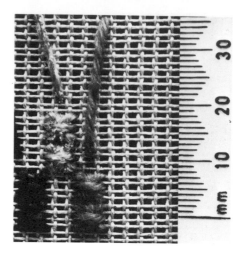

French double: 20s, 10 holes (double French): grouped warp, single weft, natural: 65 and 90 cm (25 and 36 in.)

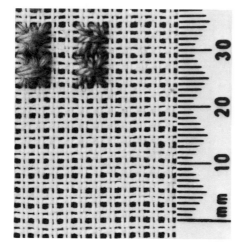

English double: 10s (20 threads): sized, grouped warp and weft, white: 50, 60, 70, 90 and 110 cm (19, 24, 27, 36 and 44 in.)

English double: 10s (20 threads): sized and flattened, white and natural: 70 cm (27 in.)

Penelope single: 18s: stiffly sized, white: 70 and 90 cm (27 and 36 in.): fawn and cream: 70 cm (27 in.) only

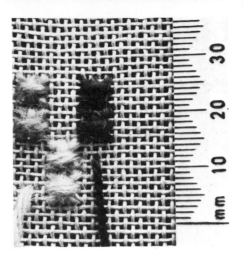

French single: 18s: stiffly woven, natural: 90 and 150 cm (36 and 59 in.)

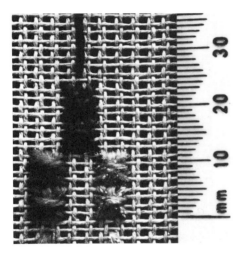

French double: 18s, 9 holes (double French): double warp and weft, natural: 70 cm (27 in.)

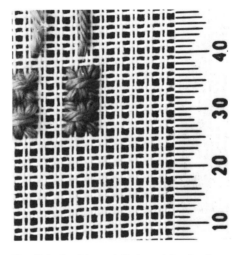

English double 9s (18 threads): sized, double warp and weft, cream: 70 cm (27 in.)

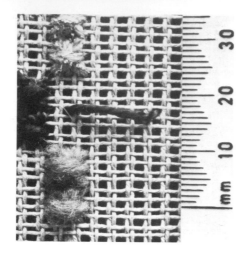

French double: 16s, 8 holes (double French): double warp and weft, natural: 87·5 cm (35 in.)

French single: 16s: stiffly woven, natural: 62·5 and 90 cm (26 and 36 in.)

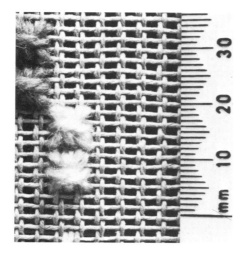

French double: 14s: double warp, single weft, natural and white: 90 cm (36 in.)

French single: 14s: stiffly woven, white: 87·5 cm (35 in.): natural: 65, 90 and 150 cm (26, 36 and 59 in.)

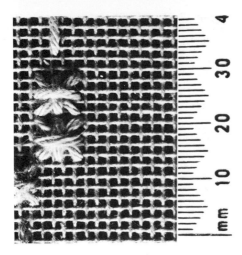

English single: 13s: strongly sized,
white: 70 cm (27 in.): natural: 90 cm
(36 in.)

French single: 12s: stiffly woven,
natural: 90 cm (36 in.)

Raffia single: 10s: stiffly sized, cream:
70 cm (27 in.)

Rug canvas double: 5s (10 threads):
sized canvas thread, white: 100 cm
(39 in.)

Yarns

The use of different yarns can produce different appearances from the same stitch. The colour and texture will also alter according to the fibre of the yarn so that great variety can be obtained from a limited number of colours. Colour modification is also possible through the combination of two yarns in one stitch. With this and the number of stitches available it is possible to achieve work of great richness.

Fish Shop (detail), Wendy Shearman
Stranded cotton has been used for the eyelets, satin stitch squares and bricking. The sheen is greatest on the eyelets and the twist of the yarn is most apparent in the squares; the bricking forms a matt background for the highly reflective diamonds worked in rayon floss. Wool produces slight relief, the fuzzy quality gives a softness to the double cross.

Fish Shop (detail) (opposite above)
The sheen of the yarn on the fish is emphasised by the use of bricking in wool surrounding it.

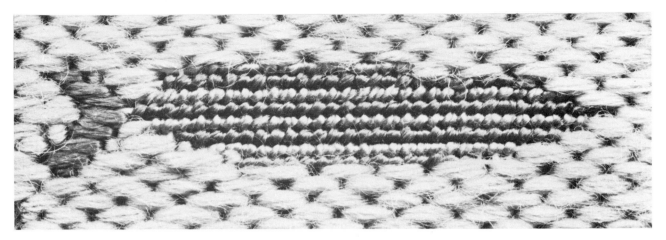

Fish Shop (detail) (above)

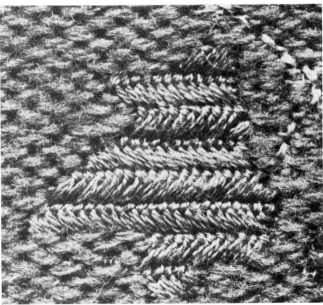

Grapepickers (detail) (left and above), Ida Russell. The lively quality of the wool in the background complements the silky texture of the stem and fishbone.

White bag (detail) (above left), Gwendolin Strafford. White and cream yarns have been used here, therefore colour does not interfere with any assessment of the yarn and its effect on the appearance of the stitch. Long armed cross is worked in off white cotton; the softly spun threads can be clearly seen. Berlin star is worked in a very white nylon which gives a soft appearance to the stitch, and parisian is worked in alternate wool and semi matt raffene.

White bag (detail) (above)
Different wools are used for scotch and for multiple oblong; the former is much more tightly spun and lifts up well with the mercerised tent between. The softer wool moulds the form of the triple oblong cross in contrast to the scotch stitch.

White bag (detail) (left)
This shows the difference in appearance of lustre and matt raffene. The first is worked with wool for a form of rice stitch called multiple rice (undulating rice), and the second also with wool for hungarian.

White bag (detail) (top)
A double twist crochet rayon has been used for these eyelets. Compare the quality with that of the yarn at the foot of the page.

(Centre left) Another highly reflective rayon crochet yarn has been used with wool in this florentine pattern.

(Above and centre right)
These two samples of double stitch have been worked with different yarns. The first has been worked with wool and stranded cotton, the second in nylon, giving a very different appearance to the wool.

Seed head (detail), Jennifer Gray
Heather mixtures were used for the
tent stitch and some of the larger
stitches, producing a further texture
which tends to obscure the structure
of the stitches; a point worth
considering in certain circumstances.

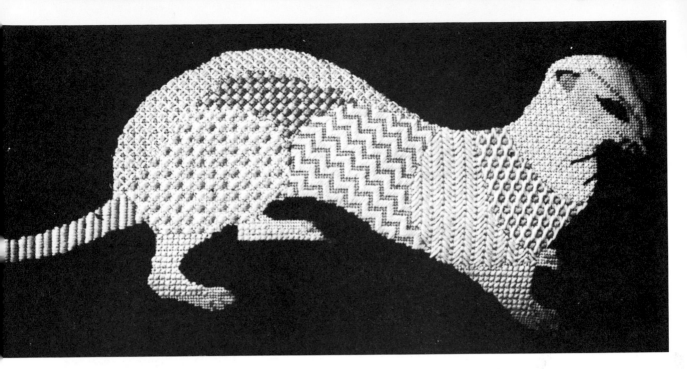

Ermine, Girton College Chapel
This is an example of a very limited
colour range which relies on changes
of stitch and two yarns, wool and
mercerised cotton, for its variety of
texture.

Below is a list of different types of yarn available, some of which may be known by other names. The canvas sizes suggested for the various yarns are only a slight indication of what can be used together. It is always best to experiment for oneself.

Weaving yarns, knitting cottons, lustre yarns, synthetic raffia, string, nylon and Courtelle knitting yarns, however, produce problems of their own. For beginners whose sensitivity to tension may be somewhat undeveloped, it is perhaps easier to start with a medium sized canvas, single 12s to 16s, using Tapisserie 4-ply wools with Anchor Soft and Perlés to give sufficiently different textures.

NAME AND TYPE OF YARN	DESCRIPTION	NUMBER OF THREADS TO 25 mm (1 in.)
Rug wool	4-ply harsh and springy. Does not compress well. Average colour range	5 double 10 single
Thrums rug wool	2-ply hardwearing, resilient and hairy. Exceptional colour range	12s to 14s 10s 2 pieces yarn
Perlita	2-ply, softly spun, high lustre mercerised cotton. Poor compression	Dobby, 5s and 10s
Rya rug wool	2-ply springy, hairy but softer than thrums. Good colour range	10s and 12s
Raffene	Lustre and matt, unyielding. Useful texture. Moderate colour range	10s and 12s
Crochet rayon	High lustre, crisply spun, various thicknesses. Moderate colour range	12s to 24s
Knitting wool 4-ply	Firm, hard yarn not as springy as Rya. Does not compress as well as tapestry	10s to 20s
DMC Tapisserie wool	4-ply about the same firmness and weight as knitting wool. Good colour range	12s to 20s
Anchor Tapisserie	4-ply softer than DMC and slightly finer. Compresses well, good colour range	12s to 22s
Anchor Soft cotton	4-ply smooth, matt yarn. Does not compress well. Limited colour range	12s to 18s
Stickwolle wool/rayon/lurex	2-ply lurex twisted, firmly spun, soft yarn of tapestry wool weight	12s to 20s
Appleton Tapestry wool	4-ply soft yarn, loosely spun. Compresses well. Good colour range	10s to 22s
DMC cotton Perlé Dewhursts Sylko Perlé	No. 5 lustre yarn, firmly spun. Little compression. Good colour range	14s to 24s
Stranded cotton	Six strands slightly thicker than No. 5. Fewer strands can be used for finer canvas. Good colour range	14s to 32s
Crochet cotton	2-ply semi-matt yarn, firmly spun. Poor compression, limited colour range	14s to 24s
Rayon Floss	Very loosely spun, highly reflective. Difficult to use without snagging. May be obtainable as weaving yarn or machine embroidery thread	16s to 28s
DMC Cotton-á-broder	3-ply softly spun, semi-matt cotton. Wide colour range. Smooth appearance	24s to 32s
Appleton Crewel wool	2-ply, loosely spun, springy yarn slightly hairy. Good colour range. Can be used double on coarser canvas	24s to 32s double 20s
DMC Medici wool	2-ply tightly spun, smooth yarn, finer than Crewel. Good colour range	24s to 32s
Cotton Perlé	No. 8 lustre yarn, firmly spun with strong twist. Good colour range	24s to 32s

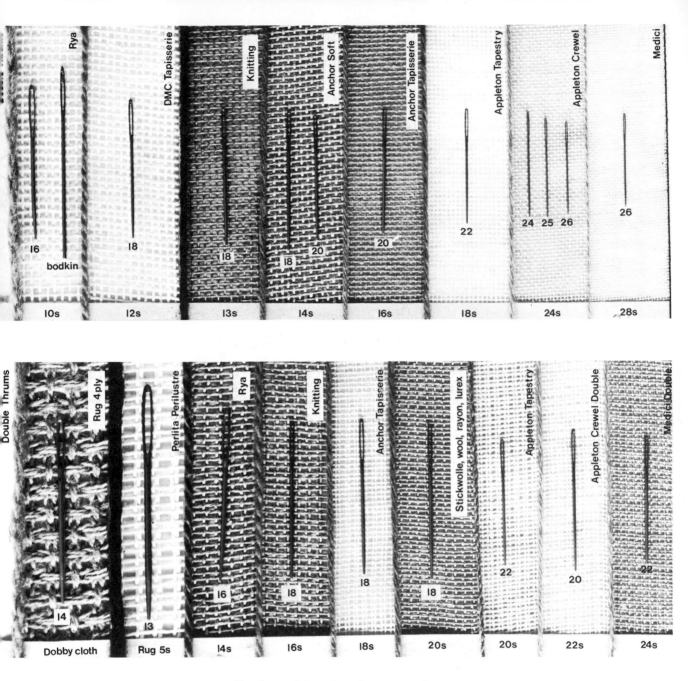

Varying weights of wool, cotton and rayon yarn have been placed on either side of canvas for which they would best be suited. Needles suitable for the weight of yarn and size of mesh have been placed on the various canvases.

Cock on Tortoise (detail), Girton
College Chapel
Again only two types of yarn have
been used and a limited colour range
from orange through pink to red, with
khaki, brown and gold on the tortoise.
The Anchor Tapisserie wool used with
Sylko Perlé offset each other effectively,
and form closely knit stitches on an
18 thread single mesh canvas.

Design

Inspiration for design can come from various sources: the materials themselves, which suggest scale, colour and texture; application of stitches in different areas and ways; the requirements of the article; and ideas from visual sources.

Repetitive pattern is a particular characteristic of canvas work. The use of material such as stacked pipes, brick patterns and ready designed material on decorated surfaces, such as ceramics, could well be used to increase the number of canvas stitches, either by the combined use of existing stitches in different arrangements or the construction of new ones. The design of this pattern, which is made up of various stitches, is an interpretation of the grill on a front door in Holland. The flattened diamond of the grill has been lost and it has taken on a Victorian flavour which might prove rather aggressive. Worked larger, the centre of the cross might have been interpreted in a more interesting way, but pattern arrived at in this way is worth considering when working large areas in a design.

The pattern in the centre of this dish
suggests a fylfot cross which could
form the basis for a new stitch or
group of stitches.

Ideas for subject matter can come
from many different sources: small,
large, natural or man-made, such as
stones, shells, bark, fruit, flowers,
trees, buildings, landscapes, water, sky,
animals and birds.

37

Bee on honeycomb, Girton College
Chapel

A good method of approach is the simplification of the form into areas in which the decorative stitches make an impact. Allow the original material to suggest the form of this decoration but do not adhere so closely to it that the canvas work becomes just a copy.

Goldfinch, Girton College Chapel

Animal, Alison Wilson
The representation of an animal in this way is ideal, as it retains those features which can be easily translated into stitches and also a highly decorative interpretation which would work well in canvas.

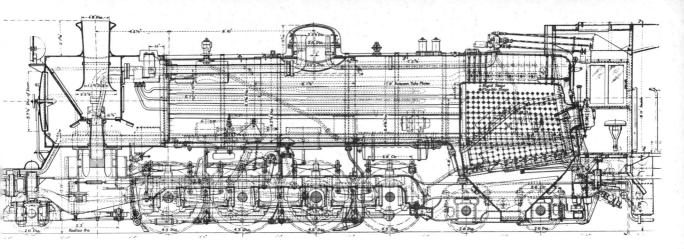

At the other end of the scale is the engineering drawing containing a great deal of detail but having an affinity with canvas work which could well be exploited.

Aerial view, Moyra McNeill
This is based on the map of a main road with fields either side. The simplicity of shapes and their treatment is very satisfying.

Stone carving from a Kentish church

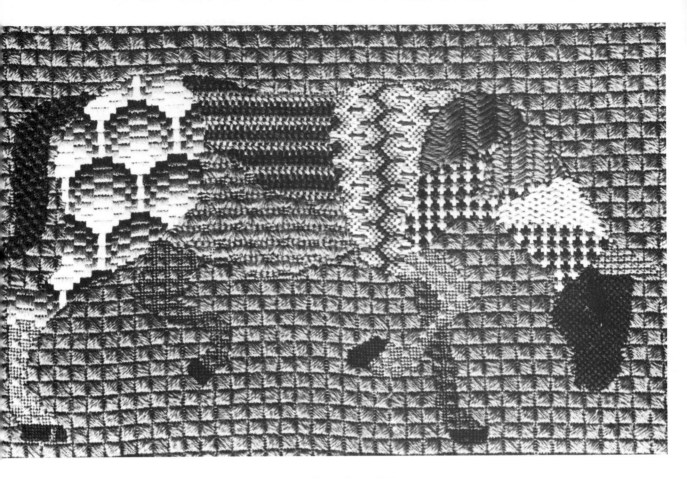

Horse, Joyce Bakes
The choice of stitch and yarn
emphasises the movement of the
animal, which has been divided into
anatomical areas. Hungarian ground
has been worked sideways following the
direction of the hide and block
florentine has been used in the
powerful hindquarters.

The Christ fish with the basket of loaves,
Girton College Chapel

Dolphin, Girton College Chapel

Fish shop, Wendy Shearman (16s canvas)
This uses a closely toned florentine in
the background so that the building
shows up effectively against it. All the
activity is contained within the
rectangle so that the eye is drawn from
the decorative house front to the
contents of the shop and back again
to the pediment.

Grape pickers (detail), Ida Russell
(28s canvas)
The figures, vines and baskets are
treated in a two-dimensional and
decorative way. The light figure and
some of the leaves show up against a
dark background, whilst the purple
grapes and olive leaves add richness to
the design.

This hanging by Mrs Howianz was
designed from a brass rubbing in a
church in Lincoln and has a simple
decorative appearance. The most
complex pattern is the hungarian point
worked on the skirt of the gown in the
strongly shaded pattern at the hem.

Cock on tortoise, Girton College Chapel
The cock, like the swallow, is worked
in reds, oranges and pinks against the
outlined shell of the tortoise which is
brown, khaki and deep and light gold.

Cock on Tortoise, Girton College Chapel
As can be seen in the full view of the
hassock, the legs, head and tail of the
tortoise are worked on the gusset.

Swallow
Designed by Jennifer Gray, worked by Anne Clark Hutchison (18s canvas). This is one of the six different hassocks designed for Girton College Chapel. The lines of the hole and nest become intermingled at the bottom edge and carried round the gusset. Dark colours were used for the hole, medium browns and gold for the nest, and the bird was worked in pink, reds and orange. The curved lines of the bird echo those of the hole.

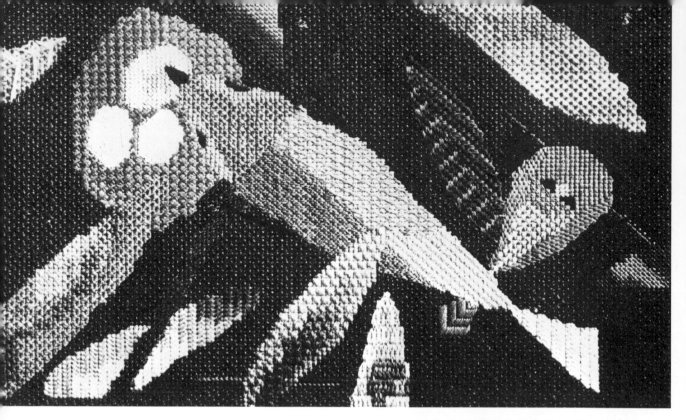

Nesting birds, Joyce Bakes (18s canvas)
Diagonal stitches fit easily into the
shapes and emphasise the direction.
The birds have been placed on the
trees very formally; a naturalistic
representation could destroy the
pattern achieved by the placing of the
shapes in this way.

One side of a case by Gwendolin
Strafford, worked on 24s in strong
colours in a variety of yarns and
stitches. The diamond pattern down
the centre is worked in one mercerised
cotton for all but the dark outlining
and is an excellent example of the
change of tone obtainable from such
thread when the stitch direction is
changed. A strong difference is also
seen in the chevron patterns on either
side.

White bag, Gwendolin Strafford
This was worked in white and cream wool, nylon, raffene, crochet rayon, mercerised cotton and beads, on 12s canvas in rows of different stitches listed below. The bag has been made up with a leather gusset and bamboo handle.

STITCH	YARN
Cross	Wool
Tied Oblong Cross	Wool
Undulating Rice with back stitch between	Lustre raffene and wool
Hounds Tooth Cross	Wool
Hungarian	Matt raffene and wool
Window Eyelet	Crochet rayon
Longarmed Cross	Matt cotton
Triple Oblong Cross	Wool
Scotch	Wool and mercerised cotton
Woven Cross	Wool
Parisian	Matt raffene and wool
Berlin Star	Nylon
Longarmed Cross	Matt cotton
Oblique Gobelin (beads in between)	Wool
Heavy Cross	Wool
Bound Cross	Wool

Canvas stitches

THE WORKING THREAD

The harsh quality of the canvas, due to sizing, tends to fray long lengths of yarn, especially wool. This can be overcome by using short lengths on stiff canvas. If two thicknesses of yarn are needed it is best to double one strand, since two pieces of yarn, when doubled in the eye of the needle, become frayed more easily as they are passed through the mesh of the canvas. The working length of yarns varies with the size of canvas and the fineness of the stitching, as it is the number of times the yarn is pulled through the mesh that weakens it. Rug wool is the toughest type of wool and being worked on coarse canvas can be nearly as long as 1 m ($3\frac{1}{4}$ ft). Tapestry wool worked on 12s to 18s can be approximately 50 cm (20 in.) and crewel wool on 28s and 24s, about 36 cm (14 in.).

THE WORKING OF STITCHES

In moving from one stitch to the next, the needle is not taken down, behind and up through the mesh in one movement, as in some hand-held embroidery, unless a ribbed effect is required from tent or gobelin. To overcome this tendency to 'pick-up' rather than 'stab', the tent stitch diagram (worked diagonally) shows the stitch being worked away from the stitcher, since there is then no temptation to pick up the canvas thread when moving to the next stitch. The use of a square frame also prevents this, as it is very tightly stretched, and one hand is above the frame pushing the needle through and the other is beneath receiving it. The needle is brought up through an empty hole wherever possible and stabbed down through the correct hole for the stitch, which probably already has yarn in it from the previous stitch. This method produces a crisp appearance to the area of stitching instead of a matted one. Where it is impossible to find an empty hole through which to come up, the tapestry needle will help to separate the threads of yarn already there, but care should be taken to make sure these are not split if definition of stitch is to be achieved.

The stitches have been drawn on a single mesh grid in most cases as single mesh canvas is more versatile than double, making it possible to work easily over an uneven number of threads. Where specific stitches require a double mesh this is indicated. Wherever possible the direction in which the stitch is generally worked has been shown, but this is just a guide to start with. Most workers find a method which suits them best after some experimenting. Three rules which are helpful to follow, however, are listed below:

1 Keep to the same method of producing the stitch for one particular area.

2 Retain an even tension.

3 Where there is a choice, come up through the hole containing the least yarn.

DEFINITION OF TERMS

Thread

Always describes the canvas mesh unless specifically described as working thread

1 crossing thread

Describes the point at which one vertical and one horizontal thread of canvas meet and over which a diagonal stitch is worked

2 crossing threads

Describes two vertical and two horizontal threads. When working over a different number of vertical from horizontal threads, the number is always given or is apparent from the drawing

Yarn

The working thread

Lustre yarn

Yarns with a sheen

Tramming

The use of the same or another yarn to pad a stitch such as gobelin

Satin stitch

When the thread is taken across the back *and* front of the work

Laid work

A method of covering a ground entirely with lines of yarn *on the surface only*, unlike satin stitch. The first thread is taken across the area to be covered, down through a hole in the canvas, up through the ncxt hole and back alongside the first thread. Where long threads may snag, another thread is worked over the laid area at intervals and couched down

Couching

Tying down a long thread with short stitches at intervals.

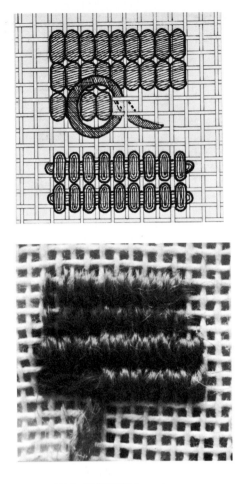

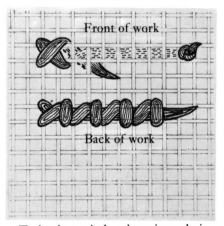

To begin a stitch, a knot is made in the end of a piece of yarn which is then taken through the canvas (the knot resting on the top) and along the back of the work. The back of the stitch then encloses the yarn in the first row and the knot is cut off. The end of the yarn can be threaded through to the back or brought up to the surface across an unworked area, so that the next group of stitches can enclose it. All loose ends can be finished off in the back of the work (if they have not already been stitched in) at the end of the working period.

STRAIGHT STITCHES

Straight Gobelin and Trammed Gobelin
(top and above)
Worked over 2 horizontal threads in horizontal lines or 2 vertical threads in vertical lines. If the yarn is not thick enough to cover the mesh the lines can be trammed.

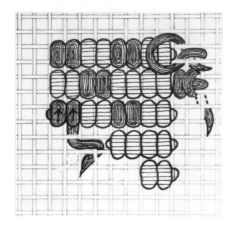

Renaissance
Composed of 3 stitches, worked diagonally or in vertical rows. The first is a padding stitch over 2 vertical threads, the second stitch is brought out 1 thread below, making sure that at this point the weave of the canvas does not allow the yarn to slip beneath it. A straight stitch is made over the padding stitch and 2 horizontal threads and the third stitch is then made alongside it covering the first stitch almost completely. This group of 3 stitches is then repeated either over the 2 horizontal threads below or 2 horizontal threads below and to the right.

Seed head (detail), Jennifer Gray
The light bars are a mixture of gros point and trammed gobelin.

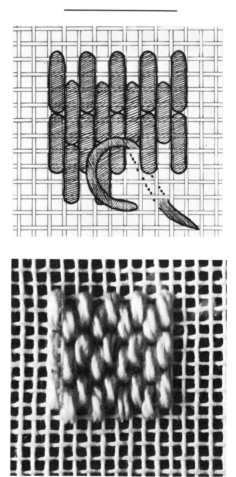

Upright Gobelin (right and centre right)
Worked over an uneven number of threads leaving a space of 1 hole between each stitch in the row. The next row is then dropped partially into this over 2 threads of the previous row and 1 new thread. If 5 threads were being covered, they would be divided 3 and 2. This can be worked vertically or horizontally.

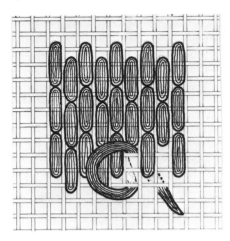

Bricking (Gobelin Filling, Brick)
(above and above right)
Worked in a similar way to upright
gobelin but over an even number of
horizontal threads. The second row
fits evenly in the spaces left by the
previous ones, each stitch taking half its
number of threads from the first row
and the same number from fresh canvas
to make a stitch of the same length.
When this is worked in the same yarn
it is worked in rows, but it is possible
to produce a flecked ground by working
a range of tones or colours in their
correct position on the canvas but in
an apparently random manner. This
flecking on orange and reds uses a
mixture of yarns as well to give a
flicker and life to the area.

Dolphin (detail), Girton College Chapel
Here the pattern of a formal
representation of a wave has been
worked in horizontal bricking. First
the light line in its correct position in
relation to the rest of the bricking,
then the medium, dark and pale green.

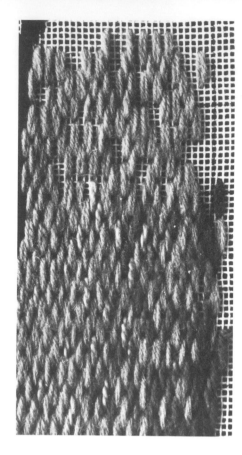

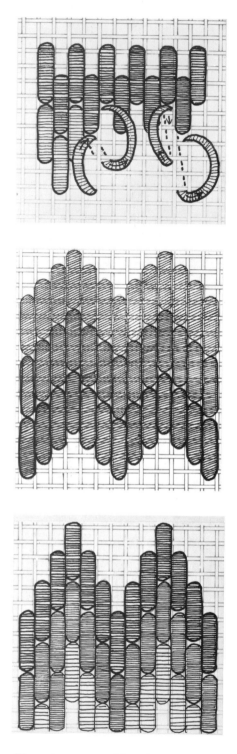

Seed Head (detail), Jennifer Gray
This flecking in orange and reds uses different yarns as well as different colours to give a flicker of life to the design.

Florentine (Cushion, Flame or Irish)
(top right)
Looks like bricking or upright gobelin but stitches are worked adjacent to one another following the intended pattern up and down. It is possible to work over more than 4 horizontal but they should not be so long that they snag when handled. The length of stitch for each area remains constant.

Florentine 4.3 step (centre right)
The first stitch is worked over 4 horizontal threads and the stitch next to it is worked over 3 of the same threads and 1 new one, so that the pattern moves up or down one horizontal thread at a time. Worked up and down 3 or more times it produces a chevron which can be accentuated by the use of different tones, colours or types of yarn.

Florentine 4.2 step (above)
Similar to the previous pattern but the stitches have been stepped up and down 2 threads each time giving a more spiky 'flame like' appearance to the ground.

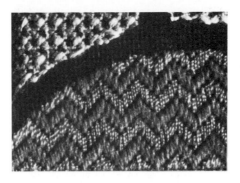

Cock on Tortoise (detail), Girton
College Chapel

Florentine 4.1 and 4.2 step (left),
Mrs Howianz

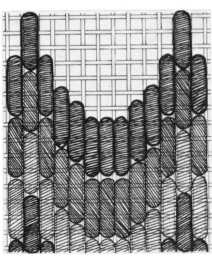

Shaped Florentine
Working from the top point of the
design this form of florentine would be
explained as 4.1, 2, 3, 3, 4, 4, 3, 3, 2, 1
step, producing a scalloped appearance
to the ground.

Owl (detail), Wendy Greenfield

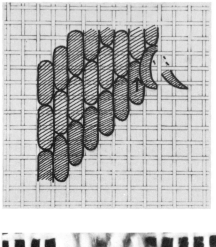

Twill
Worked diagonally over 3 horizontal threads in 3.2 step. It is worked diagonally across the area and does not return like florentine.

Double twill
Can also be worked with the angle of slant in either direction. The long stitch is worked over an even number of threads and the short stitch over half this number. The lines can be worked above or below one another.

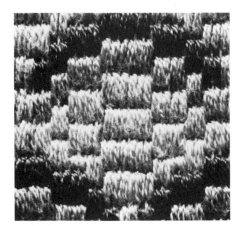

Block Florentine 4.2 step Ogee Pattern
Grape pickers (detail), Ida Russell

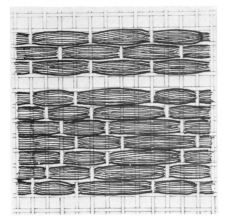

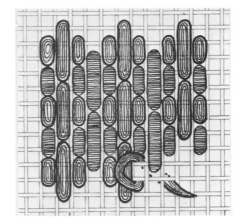

Darning

Allows the mesh of the canvas to be seen and this plays an important part in the appearance of the stitch. It is richest when worked in an evenly repeating pattern. The needle should be stabbed when a stiff canvas is being used.

Hungarian

Worked in groups of 3 stitches over 2, 4 and 2 horizontal threads. A space of 2 vertical threads is left between each group. The long stitches fit below one another and after the first row of groups, the next can be worked directly below in the same yarn. The spaces between can be worked in the same thread or in a change of yarn or colour.

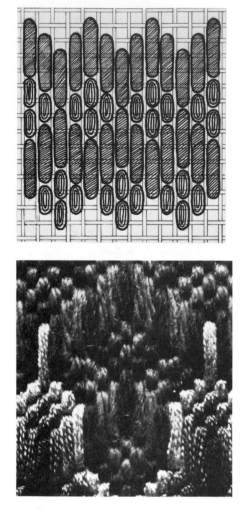

Hungarian Ground (Hungarian Point or Bargello) (top left)
Relies on 2 length stitches, one being half the length of the other, as in hungarian stitch. This is a 4.3 step, the stitches moving up and down 1 thread at a time, but because of its formation it has a very different appearance from the florentine 4.3 step. More complex patterns with spikes and curves can be charted on graph paper. These patterns are very strong, especially if contrasting tones are used, and should be selected carefully when used in conjunction with a lot of other canvas stitches in a piece of work, as their definite character may throw the design off balance.

Detail from hanging, Mrs Howianz (bottom left)

Triangle Satin (top right)
Neither a florentine or an hungarian ground but a form of satin stitch. The first row increases 2 threads every stitch until the longest one covers 8 horizontal threads, when they decrease by 2. The second row is then worked so that it fits in between the previous one, the shortest stitch beneath the longest. In this particular example this row has not been worked in satin stitch but laid work with the yarn brought up through the adjacent hole, instead of making a satin stitch on the back of the work. This produces a slightly irregular appearance with the yarn not lying as parallel as that in the pattern below.

Hungarian and Florentine (bottom right)
Have been used together here to achieve a complex diamond pattern.

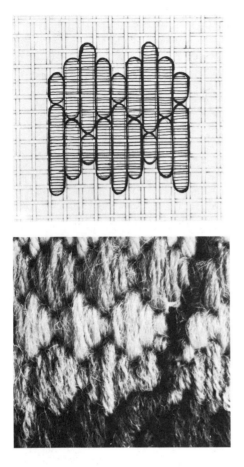

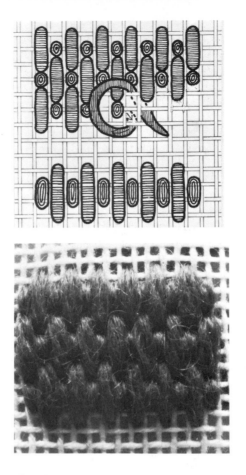

Diamond Satin
Can be worked at its widest over any
number of threads provided the stitch
is not so long that it catches. This
particular version is over 2, 4, 6, 4
horizontal threads, the next stitch over
2 making the second corner of the
diamond and the beginning of the next
pattern. The next row fits up into the
first so that the longest stitch is worked
beneath the shortest. Strong pattern
can be achieved with this stitch if
tonal contrasts are used or gentle
gradation will result from the use of
similar tones.

Parisian
Worked alternately in a long and short
stitch over 3 and 1 or 4 and 2
horizontal threads in horizontal rows,
so that in the row below the short
stitch is worked beneath the long.
This can be worked in the same yarn
or be used for shading.

Fish Shop (detail), Wendy Shearman
Parisian on left, diamond satin on the
right.

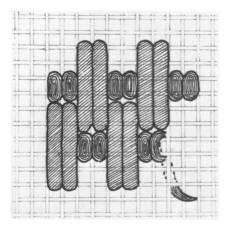
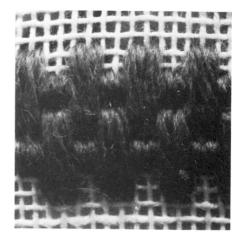

Old Parisian
Worked on the 3 and 1 principle of
parisian but everything is doubled, the number of threads over which it is
worked and the number of stitches.

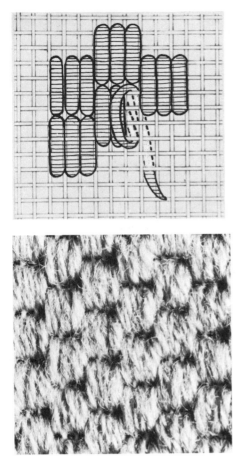

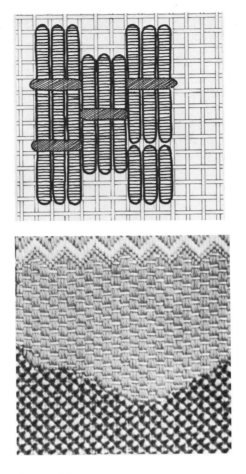

Algerian Filling (Triple Brick)
Worked in blocks of 3 stitches over 4 horizontal threads. The next block steps up 2 threads and the next down 2, so that it covers the same line of horizontal threads as the first block.

Square Diaper
Worked in the same way as algerian filling for the first stage; then a stitch is worked in another yarn between the groups over 4 vertical threads.

Alternating Squares
Worked over 4 threads in groups of 3. The squares against its 4 sides lie in the other direction. It is most effective when worked with a lustre yarn.

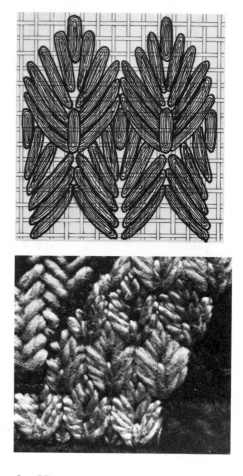

Chevron
Worked over 3, 4 or 5 threads in
straight stitches over vertical and
horizontal threads, but by the gradual
stepped movement of the lines a
diagonal appearance is given to the
ground.

Leaf Diaper
Can be worked from the top or bottom
of the pattern and the top stitch may
be lengthened to cover 5 horizontal
threads. This can make the pattern
appear rather bulky but it depends on
the weight of the yarn. The first 4
stitches from the top come up through
the mesh next to one another diagonally
and go down in a straight line beneath
one another. The last 2 large ones fit
beneath one another and finally a
straight stitch is worked over 3 threads
in the centre.

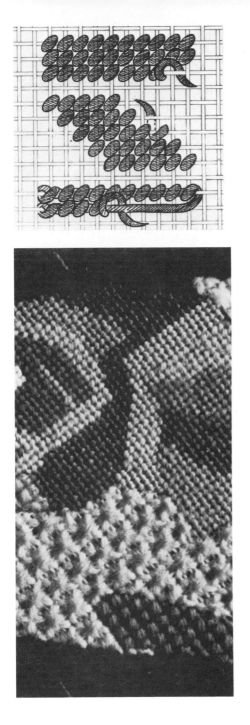

Detail from a group of figures,
Ida Russell (above)
Here the stitch has been worked in
lines as shown in the first drawing of
tent, so that the tight tension of the
canvas thread and the yarn have
produced a ridged effect.

---

yarn. The yarn has been drawn to look
slack in order to make the working of
this stitch more easily understood, but
in practice if it is pulled fairly firmly
after making the last stitch of the
previous row, the beginning of the
tramming line will be covered by the
last stitch of its own row.

Christ Fish (detail) (left), Girton
College Chapel
The head has been worked diagonally
in different reds and pinks in tent so
that a smooth finish is achieved. This
shows well against the more complex
and three-dimensional double cross.

DIAGONAL STITCHES
Petit Point (Tent) (top left)
Worked over one crossing thread of
single mesh canvas. It can be worked
in straight lines which give a ridged
effect, or diagonally over alternate
threads which produces a flat even
finish with a firmly woven backing on
the wrong side. In order to increase the
ridged effect the lines of tent can be
trammed or padded with the stitching

65

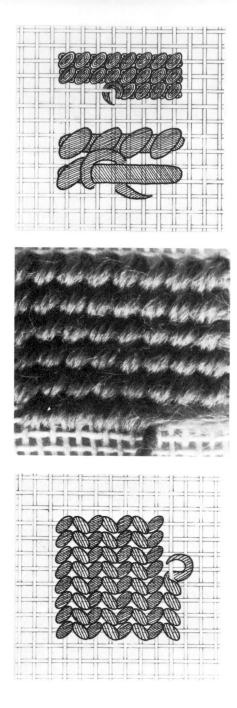

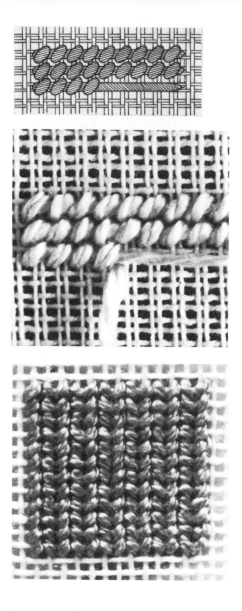

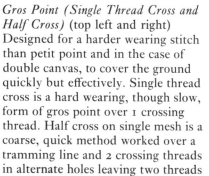

Gros Point (Single Thread Cross and Half Cross) (top left and right)
Designed for a harder wearing stitch than petit point and in the case of double canvas, to cover the ground quickly but effectively. Single thread cross is a hard wearing, though slow, form of gros point over 1 crossing thread. Half cross on single mesh is a coarse, quick method worked over a tramming line and 2 crossing threads in alternate holes leaving two threads

between each stitch. The same principle applies on double canvas which it was originally designed to cover. Here the grouped warp is separated by the needle in order to grip the tramming and hold it in position.

(Centre left and right)
Gros point or half cross being worked over single and double mesh.

Reverse Tent (Spanish) (bottom left and right)
Worked in vertical or horizontal lines in opposing directions so that if a lustre yarn is used one of the lines differs in tone. Thus a striped effect is achieved.

66

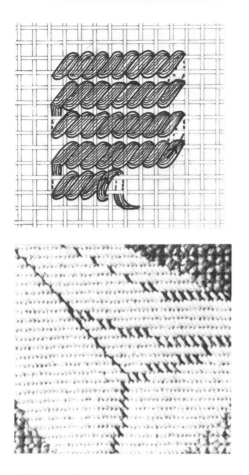

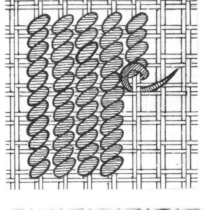

Oblique Gobelin
Worked in horizontal lines over 2
horizontal and 1 vertical thread giving
a more acute angle to the stitch than in
tent. It produces a ribbed effect and
can be padded to increase this.

Bee's wing worked with the angle of
stitch in the opposite direction from
the drawing.

Aubusson (Rep) (top right, centre right
and right)
Worked originally in imitation of
woven tapestries, in which the woollen
weft was beaten down with a metal
comb so that it entirely covered the
linen warp with yarn. It is worked
over 1 horizontal and 2 vertical threads
producing a slightly flatter angle to the
stitch than tent. It can be worked on a
single or double mesh canvas, the
single mesh giving a slightly more
regular angle to the stitch. It is worked
back and forth in vertical lines
producing a definite rib.

67

Fish Shop (detail), Wendy Shearman
Single lines of rep.

Tapestry Knitting (top and above)
Worked over 1 vertical and 2
horizontal threads with the angle of
the stitch alternating in each horizontal
row giving it the appearance of stocking
stitch (knitting term). This can also be
worked horizontally, and like reverse
tent produces tonal change with lustre
yarn. It could be mistaken for chain
stitch.

Grape Pickers (detail) (below),
Ida Russell

Waved Gobelin (Diagonal Satin)
(top and right)
A larger version of tapestry knitting
over 2 vertical and 3 horizontal threads.
The yarn is always taken behind the
mesh as in normal satin stitch, giving a
smooth appearance on the surface with
curved edges to the stitch where it
enters the canvas. This can be increased
by padding. The larger area of stitch
makes the most of the sheen of a lustre
yarn and produces a very definite
change in tone with the change in
angle of the stitch.

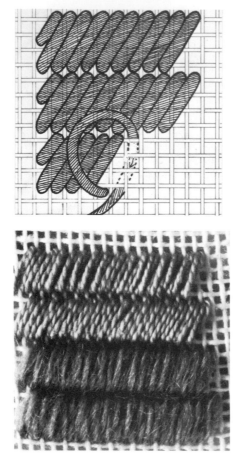

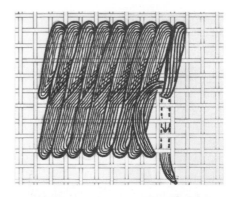

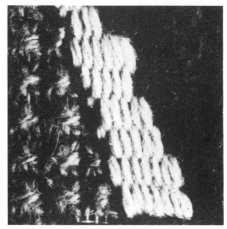

Diagonal Gobelin (Slanting or Wide)
Worked in horizontal rows over 3 or 4 horizontal and 2 vertical threads, producing a wide ribbed appearance, the smoothness of which is emphasised by the shadow where the yarn enters the canvas. It can be used with oblique gobelin, for example, to increase the variety of texture.

Encroaching Gobelin
Worked over 5 horizontal and 1 vertical thread in horizontal rows, the second row encroaching over one thread of the previous row of stitches, giving an interwoven appearance.

The illustration from *Seed Head* shows the encroaching worked at the opposite angle.

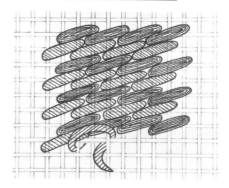

Oblique Slav (Encroaching Oblique)
Worked in horizontal lines over 3 vertical and 1 horizontal threads,

moving back 1 thread each time so that it encroaches over 1 vertical thread of the next stitch above it. The different textures of stitches make the diagram clearer, but in practice, the use of one yarn is necessary to achieve the interwoven appearance.

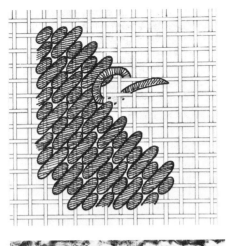

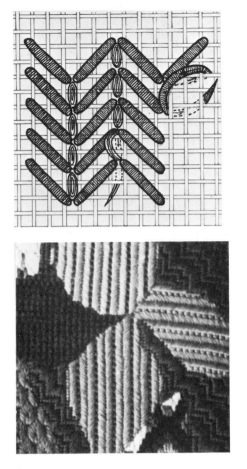

Stem
Worked over 3 crossing threads in
rows, with the angle of the stitches
in the horizontal rows alternating. A
backstitch over 2 threads can be
worked between the rows in the same
or a different yarn. The drawing shows
stitches worked in alternate holes of
the canvas. A yarn spun loosely enough
to cover the canvas may be worked in
this way or a finer yarn can be worked
in every hole. The mesh can be allowed
to show if the design demands it.

Diagonal Parisian (Diagonal Florentine)
The first name is a less confusing
term than the second, since straight
florentine is always worked over the
same number of threads in any one
area of stitching. This stitch is worked
in diagonal lines in long and short
stitches which alternate with each other
in both directions. This is another
small stitch which can produce shading
and changes of texture successfully.

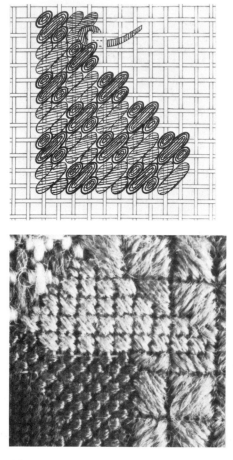

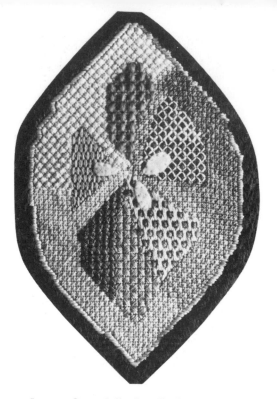

Lemon, Gwendolin Strafford
The shaded mosaic has been
introduced to divide some of the
segments. Strongly contrasting thread
or raised stitches have been used for the
segments.

Mosaic

A smaller diagonal version of hungarian
stitch described earlier. It is worked in
diagonal lines in groups of 3 stitches
to form a small square, and a space of
1 hole is left between it and the
forming of the next square. The next
row of squares fits in between the
previous one so that long stitches
follow one another on the diagonal.
All the rows can be worked in the same
yarn, or alternate rows of yarn differing
in colour, tone or fibre can be
introduced. This can be a particularly
effective stitch for gradual shading or
speckling.

Small Chequer (Checker) (above right and right)

A mixture of squares of tent and
mosaic worked diagonally in alternate
rows. The flatness of the tent stitch
squares throws the mosaic up in relief.
This can be increased by the use of a
springy, softly spun yarn for the
mosaic which can be twisted slightly
for the execution of the tent.

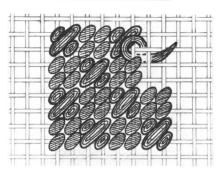

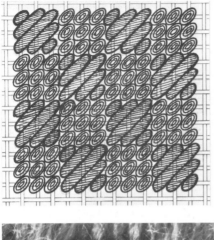

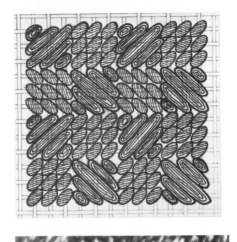

Chequer (Checker) Ground
A larger version of small chequer, may
be worked differently, diagonally-
worked satin stitch squares first and
then tent stitch. If the area is large,
it can be worked in different colours or
tones. The relief is greater than in small
chequer and can produce very rich
effects.

Alternating Chequer (Checker)
Worked either with the angle of both
the tent and satin stitch squares altering
direction in each row, or with the satin
stitch squares only altering direction.
The effect produced by this change in
direction is intensified by the use of a
lustre yarn on the satin stitch squares.

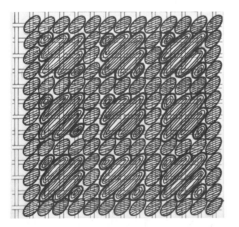

Scotch (Scottish)
Worked in separate satin stitch squares
with tent stitch worked around each

square, outlining it and emphasising its
three-dimensional quality.

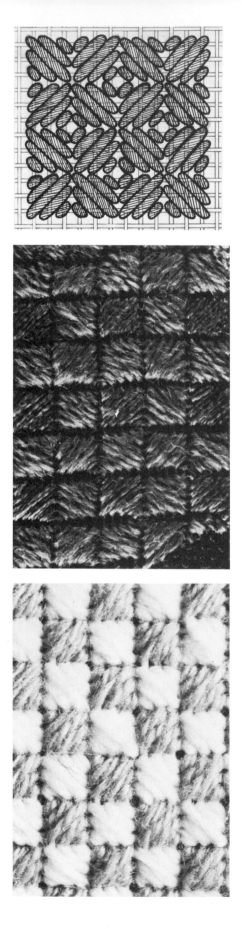

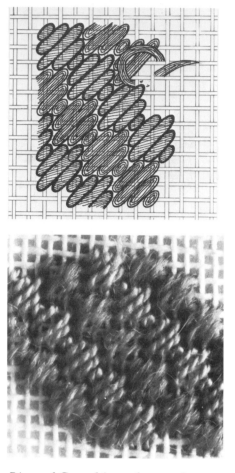

Diagonal Ground (top, above and opposite above)

Worked in diagonal rows of 4 satin stitches over 1, 2, 3 and 2 crossing threads. The tent stitch completing the square starts the one next to it so that a continuous row of squares is formed. The next row fits into the first, so that the top of the longest stitch fits into the same hole as the bottom of the shortest stitch of the previous row. These rows may be worked in the same or different yarns and this is a good ground for tone and colour change.

Flat (Satin Stitch Squares) (top left, centre left and bottom left)

Worked in a square diagonally over 1, 2, 3, 2 and 1 crossing threads. The adjacent squares are worked in the opposite direction. The slight circular movement produced where the squares meet is increased by the use of a yarn with a high sheen, as can be seen in the first of the two examples illustrated. A chequer-board effect is achieved by a change of tone rather than a change of direction in the second.

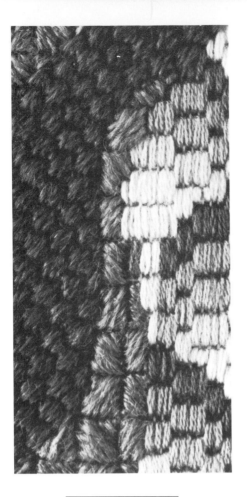

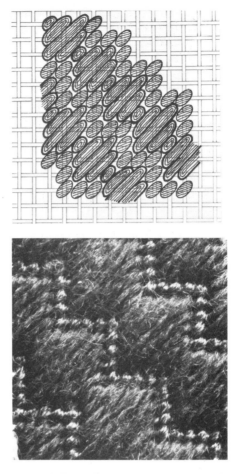

Moorish Ground
Similar to diagonal ground in the shape
of the main diagonal rows of squares,
but these are separated by lines of tent
stitch following the stepped edges of
the squares. A deeper tone in these lines
can produce a richer effect from the
squares.

Cashmere (below and below right)
Worked in diagonal lines in groups of
3 stitches, the first over 1, and the
second and third over 2 crossing
threads, one below or above the other.
It can be worked in the same yarn or
alternating bands of two or more
different types of yarn or colour. This
stitch produces a woven appearance.

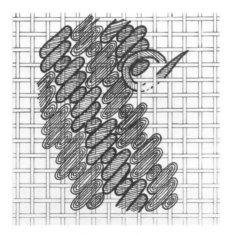

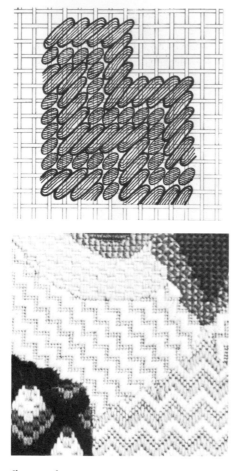

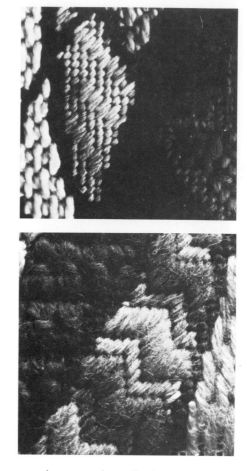

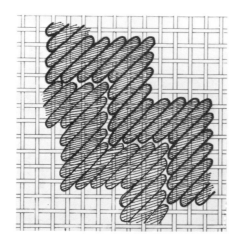

Jacquard

Satin stitch worked in a stepped manner over a varied number of threads. This particular form is over 2 crossing threads with tent stitch between. The number of threads to the step may also vary and more than the two widths of satin stitch indicated can be used. The use of a loosely spun

yarn increases the quilted appearance of this stitch.

With only a 2 step the Jacquard between parisian and hungarian is a very simple form.

The more complex character of this work is obtained by changes of tone as well as yarn.

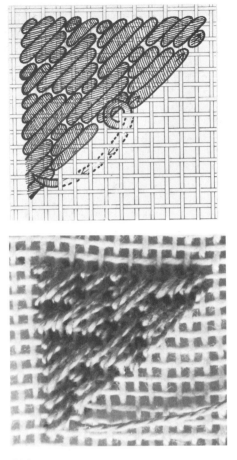

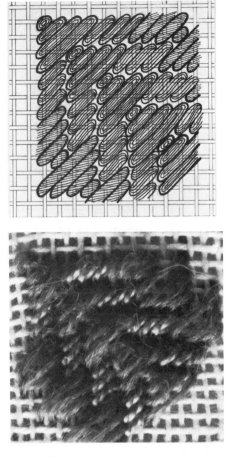

Milanese
Worked in one yarn in back stitch
diagonally across the canvas so that
the triangles fit together to make the
pattern. First row alternately 1 and 4
crossing threads, second row back
3 and 2, third row 3 and 2, fourth row
back 1 and 4. For greater effect a
softly spun wool or lustre yarn can be
used.

Oriental
The centre row of triangles is worked
one beneath the other diagonally across
the area. The 3 gobelin stitches are
then worked over 2 crossing threads
on either side of this first row and in
another yarn if desired. The inverted
triangles are then worked, in a third
yarn if necessary.

Byzantine (opposite)
Another stepped diagonal ground but
one which relies on the change of yarn
rather than the width of a satin stitch
for its effect. This particular form is
worked over 3 crossing threads but
wider or narrower bands of satin
stitch may be worked as long as the
width is constant within the area.

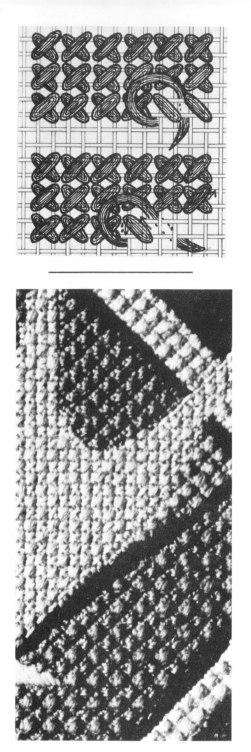

CROSS STITCHES

Cross

Worked over 2 crossing threads of canvas and can be made in two ways. In the first drawing the under stitch of the cross is worked in a line from right to left and then the yarn is brought back, crossing it to complete the stitch. In the second drawing the two arms of the cross are completed before the next stitch is made. The top arm is traditionally worked from bottom left to top right in English embroidery, in French it is often the other way round. Whichever is chosen for an area of background should be adhered to consistently, otherwise it looks untidy, unless a regular pattern of lines of alternating arms is being worked. One of the disadvantages of working the under arms first is that if the edge of the area has to be altered, the unpicking of stitches can prove a nuisance as it may mean having to unpick a whole row.

Swallow on Nest (detail), Girton College Chapel
Cotton and wool alternate in this area of cross stitch.

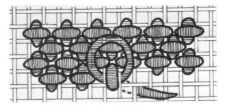

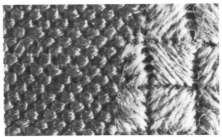

Greek Cross (Straight or Upright Cross)
Worked over 2 horizontal and then 2
vertical threads before making the next
stitch. This can be worked in
horizontal, vertical or diagonal lines.

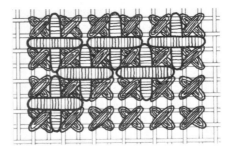

Large Upright Cross with Cross stitch
More easily worked if the small
crosses, using a finer yarn, are worked
first, and the large upright cross is
worked between in a softer spun yarn.

Fish Shop (detail), Wendy Shearman
Cross stitch alternates with flat stitch in
stranded cotton.

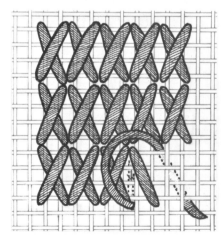

Large Upright Cross and Double Cross
Worked over different sized canvas in the same yarn. The larger version shows that a cross does not cover the mesh sufficiently so that a double cross is used instead.

Large and Greek Cross
The previous stitch in reverse. The large cross is worked over 4 crossing threads, with the Greek cross in between to cover the mesh.

Oblong Cross (Tall Cross)
Worked over 4 horizontal and 2 vertical threads, and like cross can

either be worked in two movements or completed (as shown in the drawing) before making the next stitch.

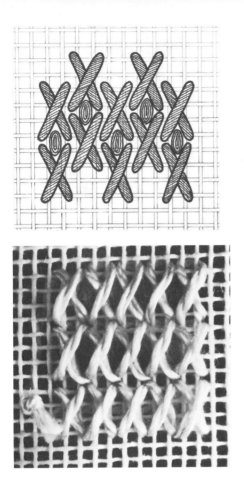

Oblong Cross with Gobelin
If a thin thread is used for this cross, the canvas is often not covered and advantage can be taken of this by inserting gobelin in another yarn or colour.

Two-layer Oblong Cross (Double Oblong Cross)
Found in a book of Berlin wool-work stitches and worked in 2 layers, the second layer being worked on the half-drop principle over the first layer.

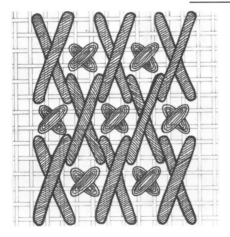

Double Stitch
A mixture of oblong cross worked over 6 horizontal and 2 vertical threads, encroaching over 2 threads of the previous row, with cross worked over

the two crossing threads left uncovered. The cushion quality of this stitch can be increased if the small cross is worked in a deeper tone.

Double Stitch Variation
Oblong cross with cross tied gobelin.

Triple Oblong Cross (below left and right)
Worked in 3 stages, one oblong cross over 4 vertical and 8 horizontal threads, a more upright cross over 2 vertical threads, and a shorter cross holding them in position over 4 vertical and 6 horizontal threads. If a space is left between, a tied upright gobelin or upright double cross over 4 vertical and 2 horizontal threads can be worked. The rows can be worked above or below one another.

Crossed Gobelin
Can be used individually between other stitches which leave a space of canvas showing, or in a block with the gobelin encroaching over 2 threads of the previous row. The cross stitch is worked over 2 crossing threads and the gobelin over as many as required or are practical.

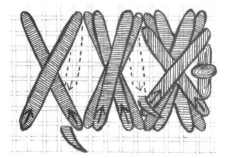

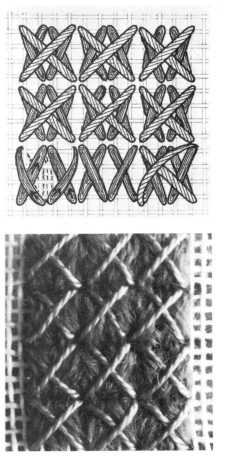

Multiple Oblong Cross (Quadruple Oblong Cross)
Like triple oblong with a final cross over 4 crossing threads tying the group together. This produces a very raised stitch, and can be half-dropped or have crossed gobelin worked in the space between.

Triple Cross
Composed of 2 oblong crosses with large cross covering in a different yarn. The arms of the oblong cross vary in direction, the lower arms being worked first, then the two top arms are worked in opposite directions, and finally the large cross covering them in a different yarn.

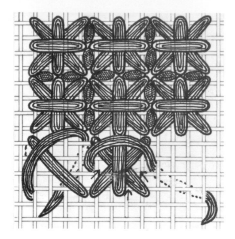

Smyrna Cross (Double Cross)
Worked over 4 crossing threads in 4 stages. The diagonal arms first as in cross stitch, then the vertical, and finally the horizontal stitch tying them all in place. This produces a very three-dimensional stitch. If the canvas threads tend to show between the crosses, back stitch can be worked between them over 2 threads in a finer yarn. The cross can also be half dropped to produce a different texture.

Imaginary Animal (detail)
Two tones of wool used for chequer board effect.

Nesting Bird (detail), Joyce Bakes
Vertical cross of the upright worked last.

84

Alternate Smyrna
Varies the direction of the final stitch either in rows or alternately, as its name suggests, to produce yet another texture from this versatile stitch.

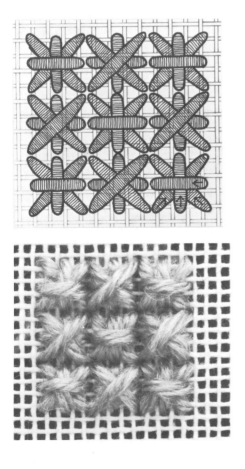

Longarmed Smyrna Cross
Either worked so that the long bar is tied with the vertical stitches, or for greater effect the vertical stitches are made first and the long bar allowed to float over 2 crosses. The grouping is generally worked in brick repeat, that is, the row below is set centrally between 2 of the crosses above. It is the horizontal form of half drop.

Reverse Smyrna Cross (Reverse Double Cross) (left and left above)
In one stitch the upright cross covers the diagonal as in smyrna cross; in the next the process is reversed so that the diagonal cross covers the upright cross. In this drawing the crosses alternate in both the horizontal and vertical rows but the differently arranged crosses can also be worked in horizontal or vertical lines.

85

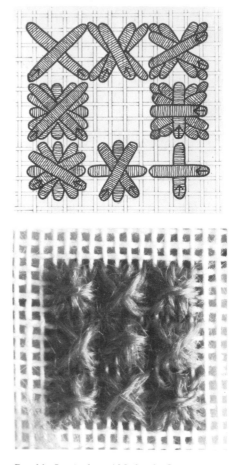

Raised Double Cross

A form of smyrna cross which is elongated over 4 horizontal and 6 vertical threads. The padded ground is first laid in groups of 2 stitches over 4 horizontal threads with 2 vertical threads between them. The cross is then half-dropped over them or, as can be seen in the right hand row, worked directly over the top. Either way, space is left in the padding for the vertical tying thread. The vertical stitch has been worked last, as it is shorter than the horizontal and less likely to snag.

Double Leviathan (Multiple Cross, Double Smyrna Cross)

Like reverse double cross is worked either from large upright cross to large diagonal cross or in reverse. It is also worked over 4 threads, but because it includes 4 extra stitches should be worked in a finer yarn. These extra arms are placed on either side of the first cross before the final cross is worked. The 2 different ways of forming the crosses can be worked on their own or together to form a pattern. It can also be worked over 6 threads.

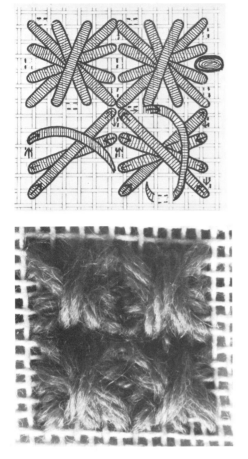

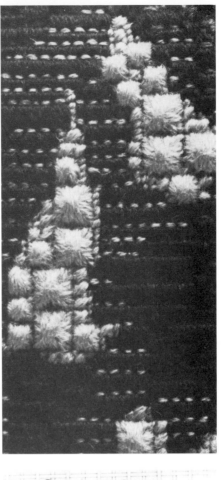

Windmill

Looks slightly similar to multiple cross worked over 6 threads but in alternate holes. The stitches are worked either clockwise or anti-clockwise, coming up 2 threads away to make the next stitch. If the yarn does not cover the centre threads a gobelin over 2 threads can be worked.

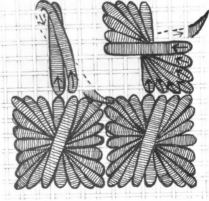

Berlin Star

Worked like windmill over 6 threads, but here a finer yarn is used to stitch into every hole. This produces a highly raised cross, the last arm of which is slanted one thread to the left or right of the vertical hole giving movement to an area made up of this stitch. In the example, different size crosses have also been used in conjunction with different width gobelin ground.

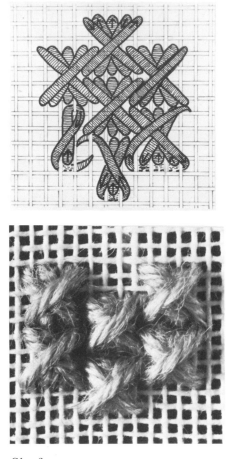

Twist

Worked in 4 stages. First the diagonal goes over 3 vertical and 4 horizontal threads, then the yarn is taken under 1 vertical thread and the second stitch is made over 1 vertical and 4 horizontal threads, entering the canvas next to the beginning of the first stitch. The third stitch is brought down and enters the canvas on the left of the previous stitch and the final diagonal is then made. This is best worked in diagonal lines.

Sheaf

Worked with a vertical stitch over 4 threads and then a diagonal coming out next to it and crossing it from top right to bottom left. The yarn is brought up two threads to the right and makes a cross from bottom right to top left. The fourth stitch then comes out one thread to the left and enters the canvas to the right over 4 crossing threads. The yarn is taken behind 4 vertical threads and makes the final arm of the cross over 4 crossing threads and the previous stitches. This, like twist, is best worked in diagonal lines. Depending on the yarn used, a satin stitch method of constructing this stitch sometimes gives a more regular appearance.

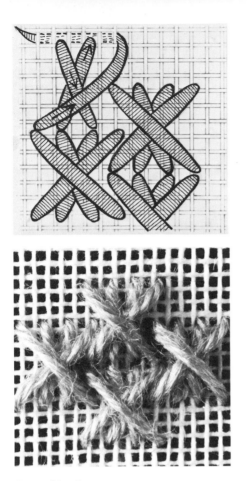

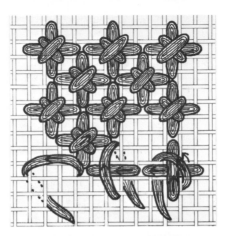

Large Sheaf
Worked first with an oblong cross over
6 horizontal and 2 vertical threads and
then a large cross over 6 crossing
threads. This is worked in diagonal
rows, the large cross encroaching over
1 vertical thread of the previous row.
Back stitch can be worked between.

---

*Double Upright Cross (Diagonal Double
Cross)* (top right)
Worked in horizontal lines with the
large upright cross over 4 threads tied
down with cross stitch over 2 crossing
threads. This stitch gives a 'pebbly'
appearance which is increased by the
use of a lustre yarn.

Swallow (detail), Girton College
Chapel
The nest is worked in dark and light
tapisserie wool and Sylko Perlé.

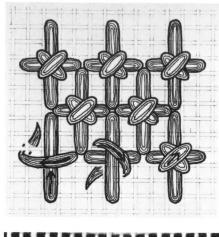

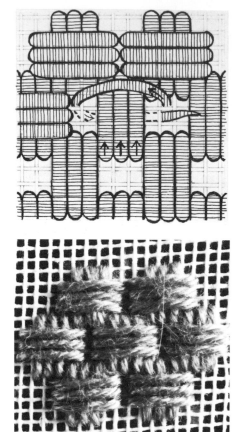

Narrow Double Upright Cross
Useful as a filling between such stitches as large oblong cross, or can be used like the previous cross to make up an area. The long arm can be any length and the short one just over half its height. If this is longer, however, than 4 vertical threads, a filling stitch will be required. A small gobelin may be needed in any case if this stitch is worked on a coarse canvas.

Broad Cross (Heavy Cross)
The 3 vertical arms of the cross are worked over 6 horizontal threads, leaving 4 vertical threads between each group and encroaching over 2 threads of the previous row. The horizontal arms are then worked in the spaces left between the bars. This produces a rich compact area of stitching.

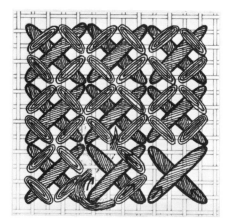

Rice (William and Mary, Crossed Corners)
Worked in 2 stages. A large cross is made over 4 crossing threads, and the arms are caught down with a half cross over 2 crossing threads. The half cross is best worked in a finer yarn possibly with a lustre, although with the correct weight it is possible to work the whole stitch in one yarn. If a second yarn is used, however, gradual colour changes can be effected by using different colours for the half cross whilst the large cross remains constant.

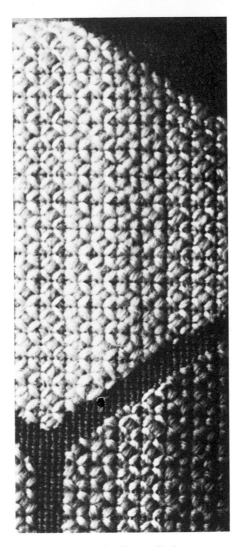

Bee on honeycomb, Girton College
Chapel
The top crossing thread is sometimes
worked in a change of yarn.

Nesting birds (detail), Joyce Bakes
The large cross changes in tone, while
the crossing of arms remains in one
tone.

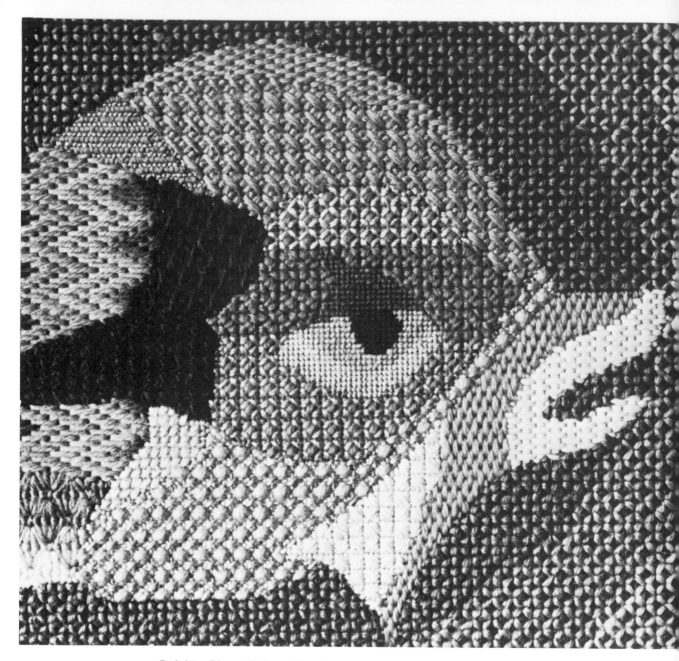

Dolphin, Girton College Chapel
This shows many of the stitches
described so far.

Slipped Multiple Cross (opposite)
A more complex version of rice. After
the large cross has been worked, a
stitch is made next to the first arm and
crossing the second. The drawing
shows the order in which the next 3
stitches are worked and finally half
cross is worked across the corners. A
finer thread than usual should be used
to work this.

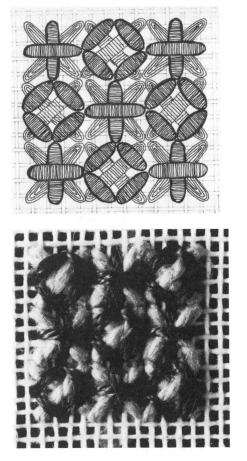

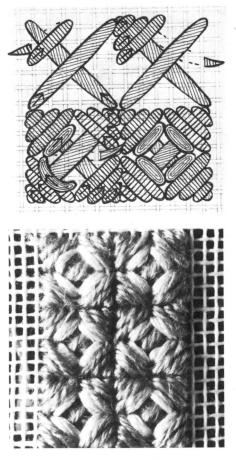

Rice and Double Cross
Can be worked alternately to produce a
patterned area if a different yarn is used
for the top crossing stitches.

Multiple Rice (Undulating Rice)
The basic cross is worked over 6
crossing threads and each arm is then
crossed with 3 stitches, the largest first.
A second yarn can be used for the final
crossing stitches near the centre which
are worked over 2 crossing threads. An
even more three-dimensional
appearance could be achieved by
shading all the crossing stitches.

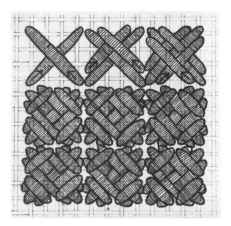

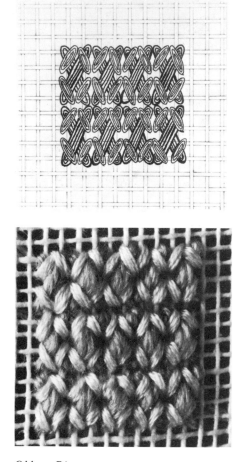

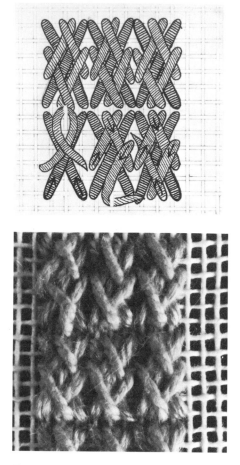

Oblong Rice
Worked over an even number of
threads in 1 or 2 different yarns.

Diamond Oblong Cross
Works well over 3 vertical and 6
horizontal threads, the crossing arms
going behind 1 vertical and 2 horizontal
threads. The plaiting is achieved by
working the crossing stitches over the
oblong cross in a systematic way so
that each one covers part of the
preceding stitch. The final stitch is
woven under the first. If the
proportion of 2 : 1 is observed, this
stitch can be worked over more than
6 and 3 threads.

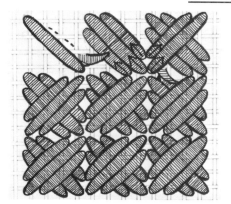

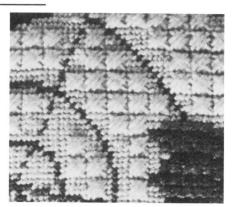

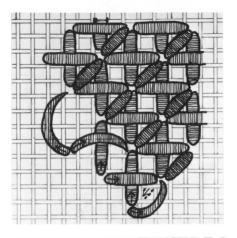

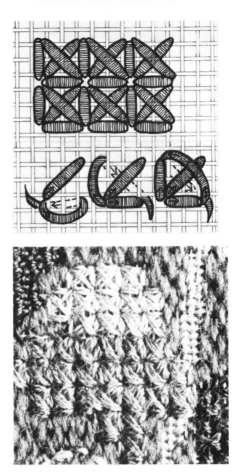

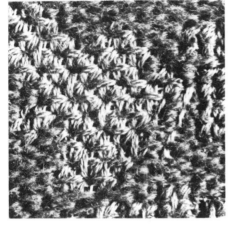

Diagonal Cross
Worked, as its name suggests,
diagonally in rows from the top right
hand corner of the area to the bottom
left. The large upright cross is made
first and then the diagonal over 2
crossing threads is made from the
bottom to the right hand tip of the
cross.

Italian Cross (2 Sided Italian Cross)
Worked in horizontal rows beneath one
another. The first diagonal, the
horizontal and the vertical stitches all
start from the bottom left hand hole,
the final diagonal from the bottom
right hand hole. This hole then
becomes the left hand hole for the next
stitch. When the area has been worked,
the row of crosses on the right and at
the top are completed with a back
stitch in the same yarn over 3 threads.
The outlining of each cross in this way
produces a 'punched' appearance
which is very crisp.

Parallel Cross (Bound Cross) (opposite)
Worked over 4 crossing threads with a
stitch on either side of each arm over
3 crossing threads. The bottom arm is
worked completely and acts as padding
for the top arm. It can be worked in
any direction and it gives a cushion
effect. The top arm can be worked in
alternate directions.
　Idea from window in York Minster
by Gwendolin Strafford.

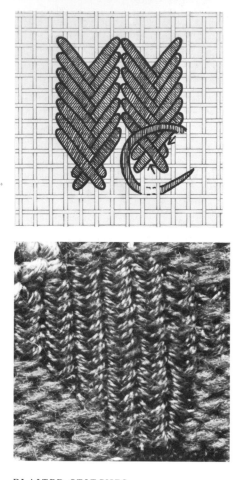

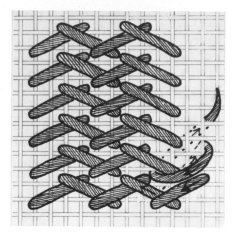

PLAITED STITCHES
Fern
Worked in vertical lines in 2 stages.
The first part of the stitch is made
over 4 horizontal and 3 vertical threads
from top right to bottom left. The yarn
then comes up 2 vertical threads to the
right and is taken over 3 vertical and
4 horizontal threads from bottom right
to top left. It can be worked closely in
every hole as in the drawing, or, if the
yarn is softly spun, in every other hole.
This particular stitch gives a ridged
appearance to the plait.

Plait
Worked in vertical rows of single
stitches over 4 vertical and 2 horizontal
threads. The next row is worked over
2 new vertical threads and 2 of the
preceding row, each stitch crossing the
tip of the first stitch so that it lies at an
opposing angle. The lines are worked
over one another up and down the
area in this manner. In the diagram,
2 threads are left between each stitch,
but if a more closely woven texture is
required stitches can be worked in
every hole. Both methods produce a
woven appearance to the ground.

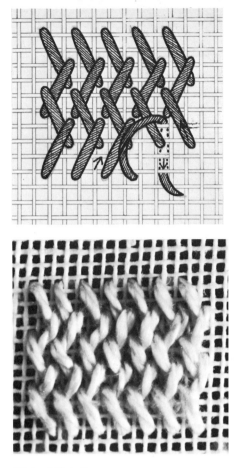

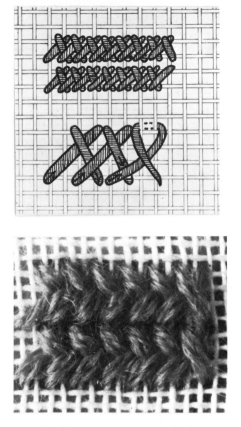

Plaited Gobelin
Like plait, is worked in rows of single stitches, but here the rows are worked horizontally. The same number of threads are covered and it can also be worked in every hole or alternate holes of the canvas. With 2 yarns worked alternately a vertical zig-zag pattern can be obtained.

Spanish Plait
Worked in horizontal lines in 2 stages. The first stitch is made over 2 crossing threads from bottom left to top right and the second stitch 1 thread to the left over 2 horizontal and 1 vertical thread from top left to bottom right. In the larger version the number of threads over which the stitch is worked is doubled. This stitch gives a different type of ridged effect to fern.

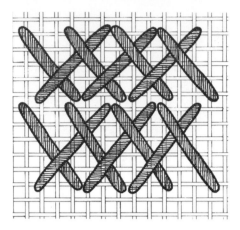

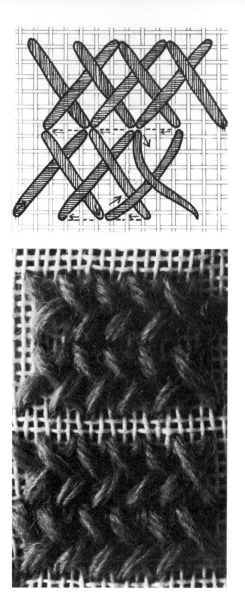

Plaited Algerian
Worked in horizontal lines in 2 stages.
The first stitch is worked over 6
horizontal and 5 vertical threads from
bottom left to top right. The yarn is
taken behind 3 vertical threads to the
left and worked over 6 horizontal and
4 vertical threads from top left to
bottom right, so that the base of the
second stitch is in front of the tip of
the first by 1 thread. The designer can
decide whether the second row of
stitches touches the first to form a
diamond, in which case the first stitch
must be started 1 thread back, or
whether the rows of stitches should lie
directly below one another so that
where the rows meet the stitches are
staggered.

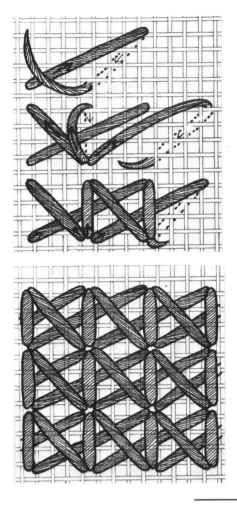

Montenegrin Cross (left and above)
Worked in horizontal lines in 3 stages.
First the long diagonal stitch is made
over 4 horizontal and 8 vertical threads.
The yarn is taken behind the canvas 4
crossing threads to the left and a short
diagonal stitch crossing the first arm
and 4 crossing threads is made. Finally
a vertical stitch over 4 horizontal
threads is made, emerging from the
same hole as the last stitch. This hole is
used for the starting of the next long
diagonal stitch. The rows of stitches
are worked from top to bottom of the
area.

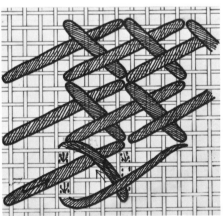

Longarmed Cross (Longleg)
The long arm is worked over 4
horizontal and 8 vertical threads from
bottom left to top right, then the yarn
is taken down behind 4 horizontal

threads and worked up over 4 crossing
threads from bottom right to top left.
The long arm is started again 4 threads
below.

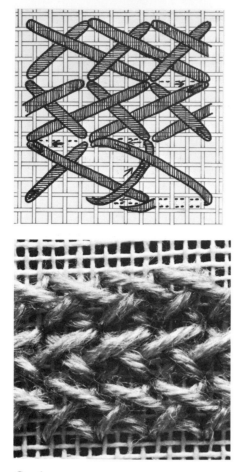

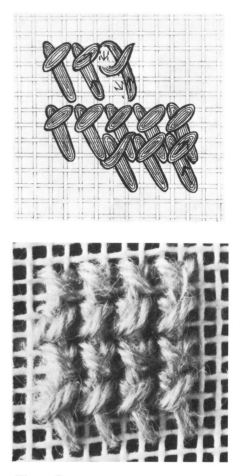

Greek

Worked first in a row from left to right and then in a row from right to left so that the long and short arms lie in opposing directions in each successive row. The smaller arm is made first over 4 crossing threads from bottom left to top right. The yarn is then taken to the left behind 4 vertical threads and crosses the short arm, 8 vertical and 4 horizontal threads to the right. The yarn is brought out 4 vertical threads to the left ready to make the second short arm. When this row has been completed, the next row is worked back from right to left, the short stitch being worked first from bottom right to top left and then the long arm from top right to bottom left.

Woven Cross

Worked with a long and short arm, first the long arm leaning backwards over 4 horizontal and 2 vertical threads, then the short stitch crossing it over 2 crossing threads. The next long arm is started 2 threads to the right of the previous one. In returning, the long arm encroaches over 2 threads of the previous row, the short arm crossing both it and the lower half of the long arm above.

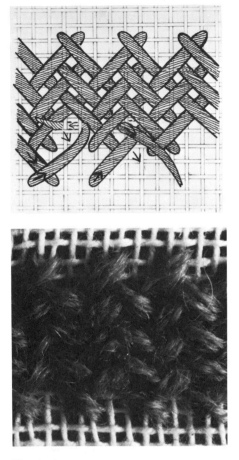

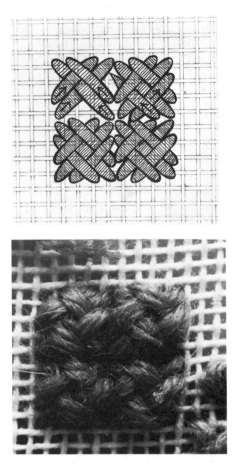

Herringbone
Worked in horizontal rows in 2 stages.
The first stitch is worked over 4
crossing threads from bottom left to
top right. The yarn is brought out 2
vertical threads to the left and taken
across 4 crossing threads crossing the
tip of the first stitch at the same time.
The yarn is then brought out 2 vertical
threads to the left ready to make the
bottom arm of the next stitch. If these
rows are worked below one another
encroaching over 2 horizontal threads
of the previous row, a closely knit
woven appearance is given to the
ground. This is a good stitch for
gradual colour change.

Interlaced Cross
Worked like slipped multiple cross in
the first 3 stages shown in the drawing,
the final stitch being slipped under the
end of the third stitch, which is also
the first crossing stitch to be worked.
The usual weight of yarn can be used
for this stitch which gives a plaited
appearance to the area.

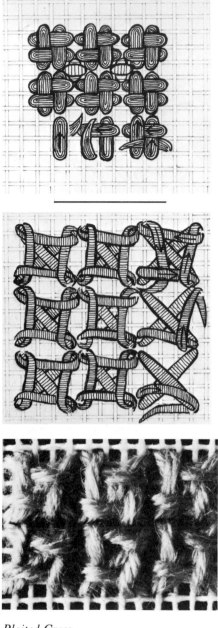

Plaited Square
Worked in 4 stages, each stitch being made over 3 threads. First the right hand vertical, then the top horizontal, thirdly the left hand vertical. Finally the last horizontal stitch is woven under the first and over the second vertical stitch.

Plaited Cross
Can either be worked in 2 stages, first with a cross and then with 4 stitches partially covering it, or if the yarn is thick enough, with the 4 stitches on their own. The cross is worked over 4 crossing threads. The yarn is brought out 1 thread to the right of the top left hand tip of the cross and into the same hole as the bottom left tip. It is then brought out 1 thread above and taken down through the bottom right hole and so on round the cross. The final stitch is woven under the first vertical stitch and into the top left hole so that a slightly twisted rhomboid is formed.

White bag (detail), Gwendolin Strafford

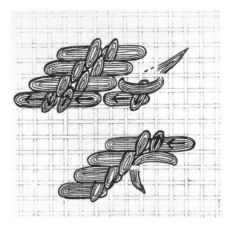

Small Diagonal Plait

Worked in diagonal lines up and down
the canvas. The first stitch is made to
the left over 2 vertical threads. The
yarn is brought up 1 thread above the
right end of this and down over 1
vertical and 2 horizontal threads,
crossing the end of the stitch. The next
straight stitch is made 1 thread up and
to the right of the previous one, and
the crossing stitch enters the canvas
through the same hole as the previous
straight stitch and to the right of the
crossing stitch. The returning row is
worked as before with the straight
stitch from right to left. The crossing
yarn comes out 1 thread below and
enters the canvas to the left of the
previous crossing stitch and into the
same hole as the straight stitch. This
produces a ridged stitch.

Diagonal Plait

Worked in the same manner as small
diagonal plait but the straight stitch is
carried over 3 vertical threads instead
of 2. It is not so ridgey in appearance
as the small version.

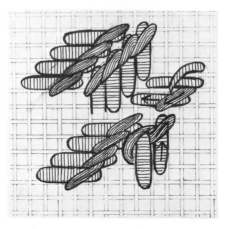

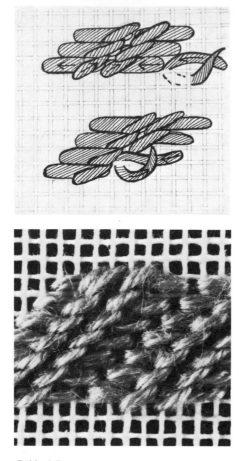

Ribbed Diagonal
The horizontal stitch is worked over 4
threads from right to left, the diagonal
comes out 1 horizontal and 2 vertical
threads below and covers the straight
stitch and 2 crossing threads to the
right. The next stitch is worked 1
thread above and to the right. The
returning row is worked over 4 vertical
threads from right to left and the
diagonal comes out 1 thread below and
enters the canvas 2 crossing threads up
and to the right of the previous
crossing stitch, so that it has to be
slipped under the previous straight
stitch. This produces a high standing
ridge to the diagonal stitch.

Plaited Chevron
Worked in diagonal rows from bottom
left to top right, then back from top to
bottom. The horizontal stitch is
worked over 4 threads from right to
left, the diagonal comes up 1 thread
above and is brought across 2 crossing
threads and the stitch to enter the
canvas to the left of the previous
diagonal stitch. In the returning row
the vertical stitch is worked up over 4
threads, the diagonal coming out 1
vertical and 2 horizontal threads to the
left and below, and entering the canvas
over 2 crossing threads and to the
right of the previous vertical and
diagonal stitch. Worked in a lustre
yarn this produces a very active
diagonal rib.

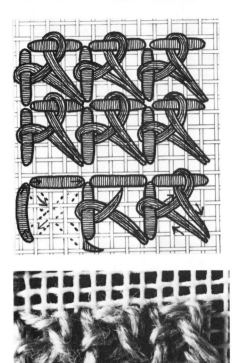

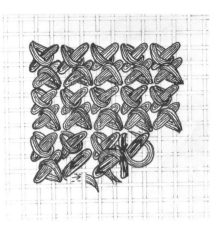

LOOPED STITCHES
Eastern
Worked in 4 stages in horizontal rows below each other. The first stitch is made from left to right over 4 vertical threads. The yarn passes behind 4 crossing threads to make a vertical stitch over 4 horizontal threads, entering the hole from which the first stitch started. The yarn is then taken behind 4 crossing threads to the opposite corner of the square, and a loop is made, first round the vertical stitch and then round the horizontal one before it is taken back through the same hole. This stitch produces an interesting texture unlike any of the other plaited stitches.

Looped Half Cross
The half cross is worked over 2 crossing threads from bottom left to top right. The loop is then made with the yarn coming out from the top left corner, slipped under the stitch only and entering the canvas at the same point. The next half cross is then made 2 threads to the right. The returning row encroaches over 1 thread of the previous row; the angle of the half cross is the same but the loop emerges from the bottom right corner. The next row worked to the right does not encroach but starts 2 threads below the previous row. This gives a small knotted appearance to the surface.

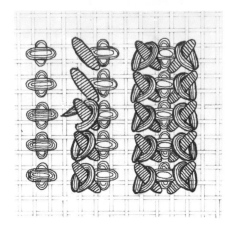

Looped Half Cross with Greek Cross
Worked in 4 stages
1   Rows of greek cross below one
another 2 vertical threads apart.
2   A row of half crosses over 2 crossing
threads and to the left of the greek
cross, angled from top left to bottom
right.
3   Loops worked over these.
4   A row of half crosses to the right
of the greek cross worked in the
opposite direction from the previous
row.

The greek cross can be in a different
yarn from the looped half cross.

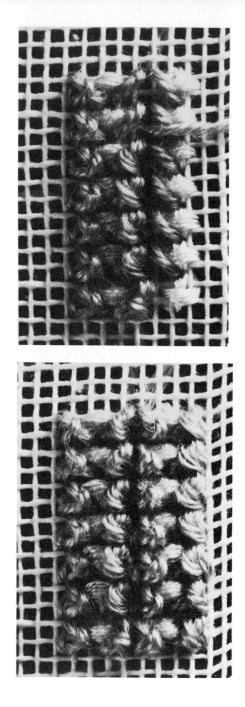

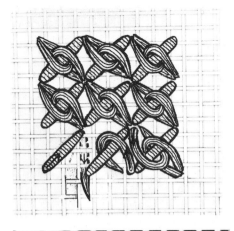

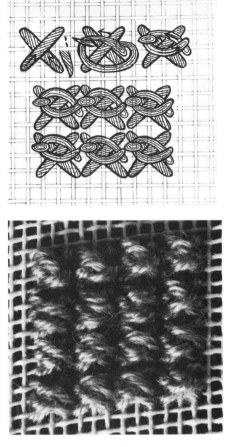

Hounds Tooth Cross
Worked over 3 crossing threads, the half cross slanting from bottom left to top right. The first loop is made from the bottom right corner through the stitch only. The second loop comes from the opposite corner through the first loop and round the stitch.

Chained Cross (Knotted Cross Stitch)
This particular form is worked over 3 crossing threads. The cross is worked first, then the yarn is brought out 1 thread above the bottom right corner, a loop is made over the cross and held with the thumb. The yarn is taken behind the cross but not through the canvas, coming out on the left with the curve of the loop beneath it. A tying stitch is then made into the canvas 1 thread below the top left corner. This gives the twisted chain a slanted appearance.

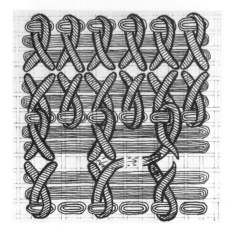

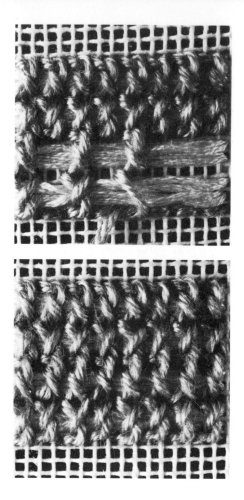

Trammed Looped Band

Back stitches over 2 vertical threads
are worked in lines 6 horizontal threads
apart and directly below one another.
Tramming threads are then worked in
pairs between, leaving 1 row of holes
free of padding through the centre.
The yarn is brought up through the
first hole, looped through the back
stitch directly above it and taken down
through the canvas 2 threads to the
right of its exit. The yarn is then
brought up through the first hole,
looped round the back stitch directly
below it and taken down through the
second hole. The next pair are made 2
vertical threads to the right leaving this
space to be filled with the alternate
loops on the return journey. The same
process is followed with the row
below, but this time the yarn not only
goes round the bar but also between the
lower loop of the first row, opening it
out slightly. The tramming thread can
be a different yarn from the looped
stitch, as it is intended to show.

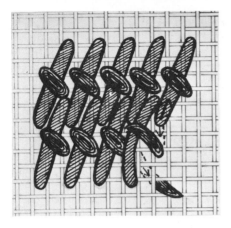

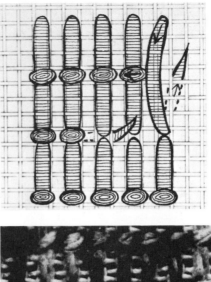

TIED AND KNOTTED STITCHES
Knotted Gobelin (Tied Gobelin, Persian Cross)

The stitch is worked upward and diagonally over 2 vertical and 6 horizontal threads. The yarn is then brought out 4 horizontal threads directly below and worked across 2 crossing threads, tying the long stitch in place. The next stitch is worked 2 threads to the right of the previous stitch. The next row is worked 4 horizontal threads below and encroaches over 2 threads of the previous row. Another version is worked over 5 threads, tied over 2 crossing threads and encroaches over 2 threads of the previous row.

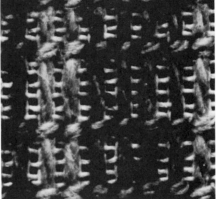

Tied Upright Gobelin (Straight Tied)

Worked over 4 or 6 horizontal threads, the tie stitch in the centre being worked over 2 vertical threads. This is worked in horizontal lines and a back stitch is sometimes worked between the rows. This can be staggered with the tie stitch.

Horse (detail), Joyce Bakes Tonal change to increase band pattern.

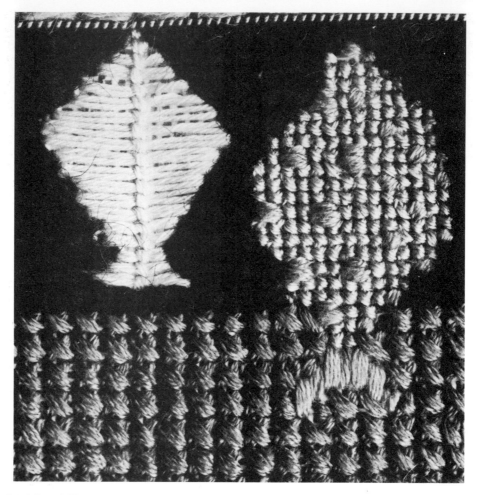

Laid Stitch Tied

Long stitches have been laid across the area one at a time and tied with a slanting tie stitch down the centre of the fish. This free method of interpreting a tied stitch can be effective if used with care so that the laid threads are not too long. A double row of tying stitches might have been better at the widest part of the fish. (Detail from *Fish Shop*.)

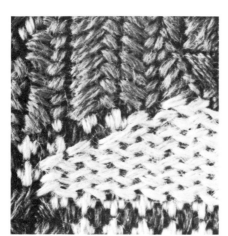

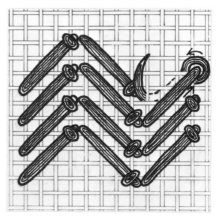

Cock on Tortoise, Girton College
Chapel
Feathers in the wing of the cock have
been shaded whilst the same type of
stitching has been used.

Nesting birds (detail), Joyce Bakes
Two rows of fishbone encroach to
form a definite band pattern.

Fishbone (opposite)
Worked in vertical lines, the long stitch
over 3 or 4 crossing threads and the
tying stitch over the last horizontal
and vertical threads which this stitch
crosses. The rows can be worked from
either direction or horizontally, and
can be placed in every hole if a closer
covering of canvas is required. For
double canvas, work over 3 and 1
double threads.

Web

A form of regular couching. The long threads are laid diagonally across alternate holes of the mesh and tied with tent at every other hole directly it is laid. If couched with the laying yarn it gives a woven appearance to the ground but changes of tone and texture as well as colour can be introduced in the couching yarn to produce subtle changes of colour.

Nesting birds, Joyce Bakes

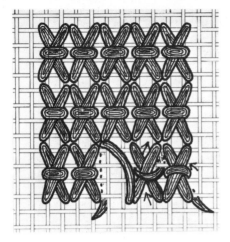

Tied Oblong Cross (Oblong Cross with Back Stitch)

The whole stitch is completed before beginning the next, the cross being made first and then tied with a back stitch or gobelin over 2 vertical threads. This stitch gives a 'bumpy' texture to the area. It can be worked in rows with gobelin over 2 threads between the arms of the crosses, or the cross can be half dropped so that the tie stitch forms a zig-zag pattern.

Oblong Smyrna Cross

Can be worked in the same yarn throughout or with the upright cross in a different one. Since it gives a tied appearance to the stitch it has been placed in this section. It can be worked over any number of even threads as long as the yarn covers the canvas.

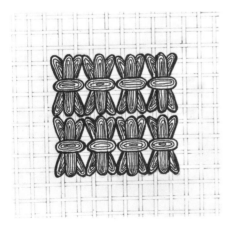

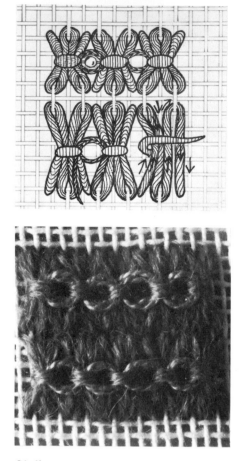

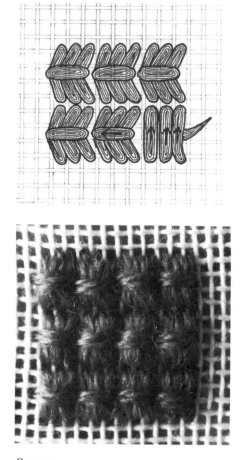

Shell

Can be worked over 4 or 6 horizontal threads. 4 stitches are made on the surface of the canvas like laidwork. This group is tied with a stitch which comes up to the left of the central thread, is worked over the stitches and goes down to the right of it. Yarn can be threaded in a circular movement between 2 tying stitches and a bead can also be introduced if it is suitable.

Smyrna

Worked in 2 stages. 3 long stitches are made over 4 horizontal threads and then these are tied with a stitch which comes up centrally beneath the right hand stitch, over the top of all 3 and down to the left of the outside vertical thread of canvas. This pulls the centre of the 3 gobelin stitches to the left giving them the appearance of the feathers of an arrow.

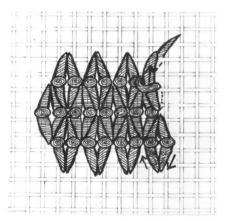

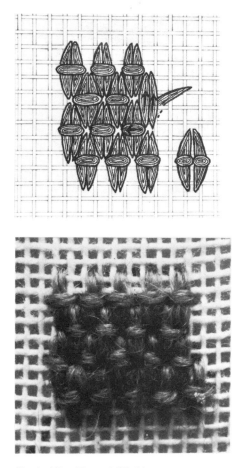

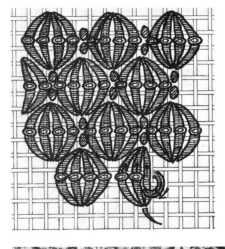

Paris (Double and Tied)
Ties the pair with 1 stitch instead of
individually.

French (opposite)
Worked over 4 horizontal threads in
pairs. The first stitch is tied in the
centre round the left vertical thread
before the second stitch is worked in
the same 2 holes. A thick yarn can be
tied across 2 vertical threads so that the
pattern covers 4 vertical as well as 4
horizontal threads. The rows of this
stitch are best worked diagonally.

Rococo (Double French)
On a single mesh canvas is worked over
4 horizontal threads, on double canvas
over 2 pairs. 4 stitches enter through
the same hole at the top and exit
through the same at the bottom of the
pattern. Each strand is tied in the
centre round a vertical thread as it is
made. The second row fits between the
stitches of the first, starting 1 horizontal
thread below the centres of the first
stitches. If the same point is used for
the hole, the area becomes too crowded
and the shape of the pattern is lost.
2 back stitches over the single threads
or a gobelin over 2 can be worked to
cover the two horizontal threads of
canvas if they show. The rows can be
worked diagonally as well as in straight
lines. When double canvas is used the
vertical pair of threads have to be
separated to allow the tie stitch to come
up between them in order to hold the
long stitch.

EYELET STITCHES

Eye (Star)

Worked in a fine yarn in every other hole of an even thread square. A stiletto can be used to ease the hole open to accept all the threads and still remain as a hole when finished. The stitches are worked into alternate holes, the canvas being pulled each time to increase the size of the hole. If a hole is not required by the design the use of the stiletto and tension on the yarn can be omitted. Always punch down into the hole to increase the crispness of the stitch; a large needle is an advantage here as long as it does not distort the outside holes too much. The tension of this stitch will tend to pull the edges of the square allowing the canvas to show, but a back stitch over 2 threads can be introduced to cover this.

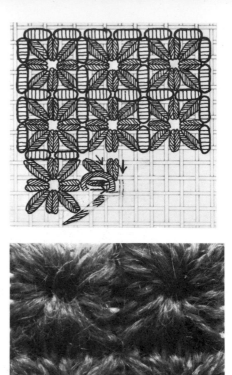

(Above) An asymmetrical treatment of Eye. The threads of canvas exposed by the tension have been left deliberately.

Eyelet (Square Eyelet)
Worked in an even square with stitches made in every hole. A stiletto can be used to punch the hole before beginning unless the intention is to fill the hole with the stitching yarn. Small back stitches over 1 or 2 threads can be worked round the outside or the eyelets can be set 2 threads apart and straight gobelin worked between.

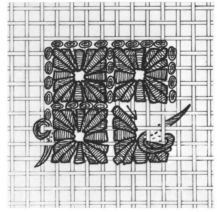

Fish Shop (detail), Wendy Shearman
Eyelets worked in wool, anchor soft
and sylko perlé.

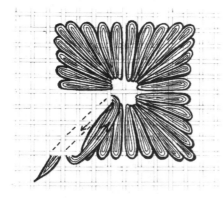

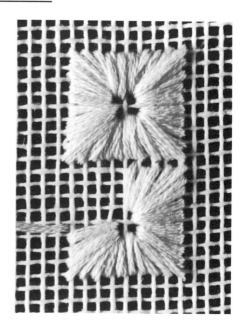

Window Eyelet
A form of ray eyelet worked from a
radius instead of in lines, to form a
square. This leaves a cross of canvas
in the centre which can be covered
with a bead or one thread cross (gros
point).

White bag, Gwendolin Strafford
Worked in twisted rayon yarn in
window eyelet with back stitch in
between. Beads have been stitched over
the central canvas threads.

Diamond Eyelet (Diagonal Eyelet)
Worked over 4 and 3 horizontal threads,
2 crossing, 3 and 4 vertical threads
round the figure until it is completed.
Since so many stitches enter the centre,
a stilletto is essential to open the hole
initially and may be needed again

whilst the eyelet is being made. A
softly spun yarn may help, squeezing
tight in the hole and opening out over
the mesh. Back stitch between the
diamonds will cover any mesh which
shows.

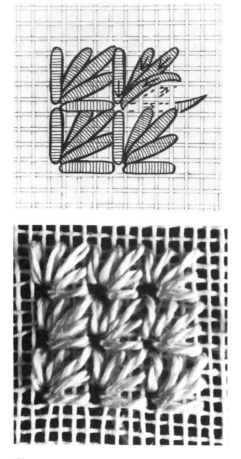

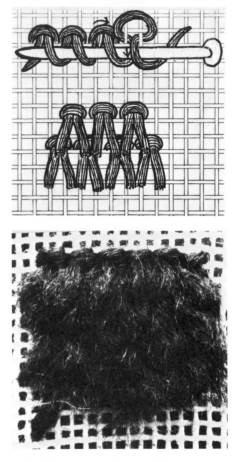

Ray

Worked with 5 stitches, the first vertically over 4 threads, the second over 2 vertical and 4 horizontal, the third over 4 crossing threads, the fourth over 4 vertical and 2 horizontal and the final horizontal stitch over 4 vertical threads. This is best worked from bottom to top of the area.

TUFTED STITCHES

Turkey (Single Knot Tufting)

Can be worked with or without a gauge. The first working thread is left free and the yarn is taken under 1 vertical thread to the left. A stitch is then made to the right over this thread and the one next to it and is brought out to the left of the second thread and under the yarn, which is then pulled firmly to make a holding stitch. The yarn is then either looped or taken round the gauge before making the next holding stitch. The rows are worked 2 horizontal threads apart and the stitches are staggered, being worked over 1 right and 1 left hand thread of the respective left and right hand groups directly below it. This stitch, like all tufting stitches, is best worked from bottom to top of the area. Springy yarn such as wool, which fluffs out well when the loops are cut, gives a different appearance from cotton which tends to lie flat and show the sheen of a mercerised yarn rather than its cut ends. The tufts of most yarns, however, can be pulled up vertically once all the loops are finished and if these are cut, the area can be shaped with scissors.

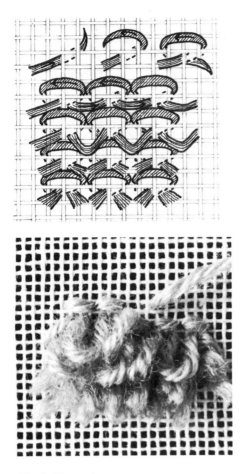

Single Knotted
Also leaves a loose end to begin with
and is taken upwards under 2 vertical
and 1 horizontal threads to the right. A
stitch is made over 3 vertical threads to
the left and the yarn brought out 2
vertical and 1 horizontal threads down
and to the right. A loop is made and the
yarn enters the canvas 2 vertical threads
to the right to make the next knotted
stitch. The pile can be left as a loop
or cut afterwards. The rows are worked
2 horizontal threads apart, going
upwards, so that the pile of the previous
row does not get in the way when
making the next.

Looped Couching
Requires 2 different yarns. One is a
strong finer yarn for the tying stitch
and the other a double couching yarn
which will relax well if cut. The tying
stitches are worked over 1 horizontal
with 2 vertical threads between them.
The couched yarn is alternately looped
and held straight and the looping lies
alternately in each row. In order to
simplify the drawing, the 2 couched
yarns are shown diagrammatically, so
that one length looks longer than the
other. When worked, they are the same
length. The rows are worked one
horizontal thread apart.

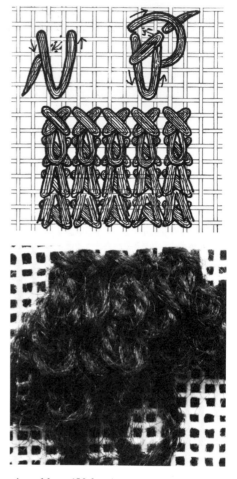

Surrey

Starts with a loose end. The yarn is brought down behind 2 horizontal threads, and leaving a loop enters the canvas 2 crossing threads to the right. The yarn then goes behind 2 vertical threads to the left and comes out where the first stitch entered under the loop. The loop is then drawn tight making the upper arm of the cross. A long loop is then made by eye or round a gauge and the yarn enters the same hole as the tying arm. Like the other tufting stitches, the pile can be left as a loop or cut, and the rows are worked directly above one another. This particular form of tufting produces a pile with a slant if the pile is left uncut.

Astrakhan (Velvet)

Worked like other tufted stitches from bottom to top of the area so that the loops do not interfere with the stitching. A loop is first made stretching over at least 5 horizontal threads and across 2 vertical. The yarn is then taken behind 2 crossing threads downwards to the left and the first arm of the cross is made, entering the canvas at the same hole as the right hand arm of the loop. The yarn is then taken behind 2 vertical threads to the left and makes the final arm of the cross over 2 crossing threads. It then comes out 2 horizontal threads above, ready to make the second loop. The cross stitches are worked directly above one another and the loops should be long enough to cover the row below. The pile can be left as a loop or cut to give a velvet pile.

List of stitches

Suppliers

Canvas, threads and embroidery accessories

Mrs Mary Allen
Wirksworth, Derbyshire

E J Arnold
(School Suppliers)
Butterley Street, Leeds

Art Needlework Industries Ltd
7 St Michael's Mansions
Ship Street
Oxford

Craftsman's Mark Ltd
Broadlands, Shortheath
Farnham, Surrey

Harrods Ltd
Brompton Road
Knightsbridge, London SW1

T M Hunter
Sutherland Wool Mills
Brora, Sutherland

J Hyslop, Bathgate and Company
Victoria Works, Galashiels

Hugh Mackay and C Ltd
Freemen Place, Durham City

Mace and Nairn
89 Crane Street,
Salisbury, Wiltshire

Royal School of Needlework
25 Princes Gate
South Kensington, London

Christine Riley
53 Barclay Street, Stonehaven
Kincardineshire AB3 2AR

Mrs Joan L Trickett
110 Marsden Road
Burnley, Lancashire

Many local handicraft shops supply rug canvas and some finer canvas. Some embroidery departments in large stores supply 16s or 18s single and double canvas

UNITED STATES

Canvas threads and embroidery accessories

American Crewel Studio
Box 553 Westfield
New Jersey 07091

American Thread Corporation
90 Park Avenue, New York

Appleton Brothers of London
West Main Road, Little Compton
Rhode Island 02837

Bucky King Embroideries Unlimited
121 South Drive
Pittsburgh, Pennsylvania 15238

The Needle's Point Studio
1626 Macon Street, McLean
Virginia 22101

Paternayan Bros
312 East 95th Street
New York, NY 10028

Yarn Bazaar
Yarncrafts Ltd
3146 M Street
North West Washington DC

Squared canvas and graph paper

Eric H Greene and Co
11044 Weddington Street
PO Box 257
North Hollywood
California 91603

also obtainable through

William Brandt and Co Ltd
PO Box 1400
112 Lichfield Street
Christchurch, New Zealand

Coats Patons (Australia) Limited
321-355 Ferntree Gully Road
PO Box 110, Mount Waverley
Victoria, Australia

S R Kertzer and Co Ltd
257 Adelaide Street West
Toronto 129, Ontario, Canada

Raffles Agencies
45-48 Canada House
90 President Street
Johannesburg, South Africa

Book list

Encyclopedia of Needlework, Therese de Dilmont, DMC Alsacc

Embroidery in Religion and Ceremonial, Beryl Dean, Batsford London

Canvas Embroidery, Diana Springall, Batsford London, Branford Massachusetts

Canvas Work from the Start, Anne Dyer and Valerie Duthoit, Bell London

Samplers and Stitches, Mrs Archibald Christie, Batsford London

Ideas for Canvas Work, Mary Rhodes, Batsford London